The Book of Raci

THE BOOK OF RACING QUOTATIONS

Nick Robinson and David Llewellyn

Stanley Paul
London Sydney Auckland Johannesburg

Stanley Paul & Co. Ltd

An imprint of Century Hutchinson Ltd

62–65 Chandos Place, London WC2N 4NW

Century Hutchinson Australia (Pty) Ltd
89–91 Albion Street, Surry Hills, NSW 2010

Century Hutchinson New Zealand Limited
PO Box 40–086, Glenfield, Auckland 10

Century Hutchinson, South Africa (Pty) Ltd
PO Box 337, Bergvlei 2012, South Africa

First published 1988

© Nick Robinson and Sir David Llewellyn 1988

Set in Linotron Times by Input Typesetting Ltd

Printed and bound in Great Britain by
Anchor Brendon Ltd

ISBN 0 09 172714 6

Contents

Introduction

Racing is fortunate to have always had an abundance of talented writers to comment on the fortunes of the Turf. Some of these have already made their mark in other areas of journalism, and have been drawn to the game by their enjoyment, love and interest in it. Other outstanding writers have come from within racing itself: people like Dick Francis and Brough Scott being just two examples.

The majority of my quotations have been taken from the pages of *Pacemaker International* from 1974 to 1988, and I owe an enormous debt to all those writers who contributed to our pages over that period, particularly in the early years when we were struggling for survival and our fees could hardly have been called over-generous!

In particular I would like to acknowledge the contributions of Jeffrey Bernard, Colin Fleetwood-Jones, Paul Haigh, Juliette Harrison, Ivor Herbert, James Lambie, Roger Mortimer, Peter O'Sullevan, Christopher Poole, Jonathan Powell, Brough Scott, Julian Wilson, Noel Winstanley and Howard Wright.

To others I owe a more specific debt – to Tim Fitzgeorge-Parker, who for many years was *Pacemaker*'s Correspondent-in-Chief, and to Michael Harris, who was my editor from 1974 until 1988.

Finally my thanks to Sarah Chidgey for her help in compiling these quotes into some sort of order.

Nick Robinson

It did not occur to me that one day my random files, culled in the main from *The Sporting Life* over twenty years, would ever run the gauntlet of publication. Otherwise I would have taken more care to identify sources. Making good defects has been a penance; and if any faults remain, I ask absolution from the many gifted writers who have made British racing journalism supreme in the world.

If it is too romantic to claim that we alone have been 'the music makers' and 'the dreamers of dreams', I cannot think of one major advance on the Turf which has been made without us. My own choice of quotations may well lay too much stress on this achievement and too little on the contribution of the forces of conservatism. But the contrast needs to be made, provided we bear in mind the cautionary words of John Hislop that opinion in racing tends towards extremes.

I owe special thanks to Monty Court for permission to repeat quotations which, for the most part, have been taken from *The Sporting Life*, to Ossie Fletcher, who gave me my chance, to Graham Taylor and to all my colleagues, past and present, who have sustained me over many years – with scarcely a ripple on the water. Our Turf is notoriously schismatic. Nonetheless I have received from friend and adversary alike nothing but help and encouragement and I am most grateful.

I thank too most warmly Doreen Handby for her skill, patience and kindness over many years which have made possible my share in this anthology.

David Llewellyn

Photographic acknowledgement

For permission to reproduce copyright photographs, the authors and publishers would like to thank Sport & General, Central Press, Tony Edenden, Press Association, Gerry Cranham, George Selwyn, Sporting Pictures (UK) and John Macnee.

1
Racing

The Derby is the Blue Riband of the Turf.

DISRAELI in *Life of George Bentinck*.

It is said that all those who go racing are rogues and vagabonds. That may not be true. But it is true that all rogues and vagabonds go racing.

SIR ABE BAILEY in *Memoirs of Jack Fairfax-Blakeborough*.

If I were to begin my life again, I would go to the Turf for friends. They seem to me to be the only people who really hold close together. It may be that each knows something that might hang the other – but the effect is altogether delightful.

LADY ASHBURTON in *Memoirs of Jack Fairfax-Blakeborough*.

When Elgar composed his violin concerto he asked Yehudi Menuhin, then a boy, to come down to the West country and play it with an orchestra conducted by himself. They played it straight through, without a break. Then Elgar said: 'That'll do. Now we can go to the races.'

BOOTHBY in *Recollections of a Rebel*.

For good undone, and gifts misspent, and resolutions vain
'Tis somewhat late to trouble: this I know–
I should live the same life over, if I had to live again;
And the chances are I go where most men go.

ADAM LINDSAY GORDON, amateur rider.

Trainer to Panamanian jockey at a Florida track;
  'Why did you ride so wide at the bend?'
  'I had to – there was an alligator on the track.'

JULIAN WILSON in *Win at Flat Racing with the Experts*.

No film director planning a new *Mr Chips* could have dreamt up
a more spectacular final shot than the view of R. B., his head and
one waving hand just visible above an ocean of cheering boys,
against the backdrop of Lupton's Tower, with the pale faces of
the Fellows, who had been meeting over dinner, peering out of
its upper windows at a demonstration of affection that they could
scarcely credit. And, walking away from this magical scene the son
of a well-known Irish racehorse trainer, impervious to hysteria,
remarked to one of the younger masters, 'What a very tedious
episode!'

ROBERT BIRLEY'S farewell to the boys at Eton, *Red Robert*.

If there is any industry involving millions of pounds and thousands
of men in which everything is all right, it ought to be stuffed and
put on exhibition.

JACK LEACH in *A Rider on the Stand*.

I'm a bloody pro. I'm a master of my art . . . and nobody can
take that away. You won't find me knocking English racing – it's
the straightest and fairest in the world.

RYAN PRICE.

Opinion on the Turf tends to extremes.

JOHN HISLOP, *The British Racehorse*, **1970**.

In racing to insult a man's horse is worse than insulting his wife.

JOHN OAKSEY.

There is a danger of racing losing the charm it once possessed as
a sport and of becoming just a cold-blooded business, seemingly
dedicated to the dreary objective of making rich men even richer.

ROGER MORTIMER, *The Racehorse*, **1972**.

Fear is complete imagination. Look at all the people who go around frightened of dying, worrying whether they are going to serve in heaven or rule in hell. If only they'd realize that you only go to heaven for the climate and to hell for the company.

EDDIE MAGNER, *The Racehorse*, 1973.

The best thing to do with horse racing in this country is to get rid of it. I don't know a more pointless pursuit.

MICHAEL BARRATT, 'Any Questions', BBC, 1974.

No doubt there are those in television management who would not mourn the passing of television coverage on its present scale. It would, after all, be cheaper – and more dependable – to transmit an old movie on Saturday afternoon. In most cases the audience would not fall.

JULIAN WILSON, 1974.

People are always going to sail close to the wind and the raffish excitement that something might have what the Irish call 'a little drop of improvement about him' is part of racing's attraction.

BROUGH SCOTT.

The sport of steeplechasing will remain a dangerous pursuit for the participants for as long as it provides an invigorating spectacle for those who watch. The object is to lessen the dangers but not the spectacle and there is still some headway to be made along this tricky course.

A doctor, *Pacemaker*, 1975.

The two mysteries of the Turf are, firstly, how there are so many owners, and, secondly, how trainers survive year after year.

CHRISTOPHER COLLINS, *Pacemaker*, 1975.

In the beginning this game [racing] was an exercise for those people, namely the aristocracy, who rode down to the course on their hacks. It was almost a kind of circus in the Roman sense with the riff-raff allowed to attend on sufferance.

PHIL BULL, 1975.

Racing's all very well if you're a success, but it's never going to owe anyone a living. If I had a son I wouldn't let him touch it with a barge pole.

GRAHAM THORNER, quoted by Brough Scott, in the *Sunday Times*, **1976**.

Racing's only a piddling little pond really.

PHIL BULL, quoted by Brough Scott in the *Sunday Times*, **1977**.

Obviously you would not expect us to say we would mind if greyhound racing disappeared in favour of horses.

DAME ELIZABETH ACKROYD, to the Royal Commission on Gambling, **1977**.

Racing is like fishing: it's the one that gets away that fascinates and intrigues.

ROBERT MORLEY, actor, **1977**.

Racing over the last twenty years has been uncertain of the fact that it is an entertainment and, like the theatre, it has a duty to entertain the public.

REG GRIFFIN, *Timeform* managing director, at the St Leger Dinner, **1978**.

Like all the big handicaps, the Ebor isn't what it used to be! The Turf authorities denigrate handicaps and have seen to it that they can no longer be endowed with prize money such as might tend to make them a challenge to the importance of the official pattern races.

Timeform's Racehorses of 1979.

If I were Major Wyatt, rather than being credited with having introduced graded racing, I would quietly draw a veil over it.

WALTER GLYNN, *The Racehorse*, **1979**.

Why, for instance, should not the Cheltenham Gold Cup and Kempton's King George VI Chase be run at a level 11st, instead of, as now, up to a stone more? At such a weight, every horse would find itself divested of a stone of lead: nor would such a racing weight present problems to any of the professional jockeys.

It is purely tradition, I suspect, that makes those who control our steeplechasing look with horror at such a suggestion. But if, as it now seems, we are not breeding the type of chaser capable of carrying 12st at the tremendous pace at which even three-mile chases are now run, without imposing too great a strain on legs and feet, then it is surely better to reduce the weights to be carried.

TOM NICKALLS, *The Field*.

Racing is part of the leisure industry combined with an element of husbandry. Both require selling and promotion. This is where unit costs come in. It may upset the traditionalists, but suppose you run eight races a day instead of the usual six. You give the racegoers better value for money – more races per pound. The bookmakers have a better chance, the Tote overheads are reduced, catering costs are better spread. You reduce your unit costs. Just like seats in aircraft.

SIR FREDDIE LAKER.

It has been said that racing is classless only in the sense of bringing together the worst elements of every class.

GEOFFREY WHEATCROFT, *Sunday Telegraph*, **1980**.

I believe that, whatever we do, we should always remember two things. First, racing is about horses and, secondly, it must be fun.

JOHN MACDONALD-BUCHANAN, ex-senior steward, **1980**.

I would say the most important attributes in racing are honesty number one, organization number two and knowledge number three.

LORD HARRINGTON, **1984**.

Racing is about everybody having a chance.

MAURICE CAMACHO, **1985**.

The sport is also a business, but above all else it's a business to be enjoyed, and at a time when the public interest in racing, both in newspapers and on television, is being questioned as never before, some Gifford-style warmth and enthusiasm must come through. For Macer Gifford left a message. It's not just performance that counts. It's people.

BROUGH SCOTT, *Sunday Times*, **1985**.

With jockeys the size of well-fed bookmakers and horses disqualified for breaking into a gallop, even the Chinese didn't want to know.

MONTY COURT, The *Weekender*, **1985**, on Woodrow Wyatt's short-lived love affair with trotting.

Not so much trophies, but souvenirs of a shoddy rip-off.

MONTY COURT, The *Weekender*, **1985**, on 'trophies' being forced on winning owners.

Unfortunately, racing is very fragmented and everybody is concerned with their own interests. So many times they seem to be pulling against each other, rather than working together for the good of racing as a whole. It applies to every section of the industry, and racegoers are as guilty as the rest.

MARK KERSHAW, clerk of the course at Epsom, **1985**.

The whole sport is based on optimism. You've got to be able to lose with a smile and feel you're going to win tomorrow.

CHARLES WILSON, editor of *The Times*, **1986**.

Racing can't *not* have a crowd problem. Part of the fun is carousing.

BROUGH SCOTT, **1986**.

There is a glorious absurdity about racing.

BROUGH SCOTT.

It's a comradely, sporting world in which people seldom complain about misfortune. Some of them may be hot, but few are unpleasant.

LORD WYATT, chairman of the Tote, **1986**.

If some horses merit *Timeform*'s dreaded double squiggle for terrible performances what about the men responsible for The Mr Chris Real Dairy Cream Cake Handicap Hurdle?

MONTY COURT The *Weekender* **1986**, on the subject of sponsors giving races terrible names.

In the beginning was not the Levy. In the beginning was racing, and it managed for three centuries without a levy.

SIR IAN TRETHOWAN, chairman of the Horserace Betting Levy Board, **1987**.

We need radical change in the Pattern Race System, whose tail has been wagging racing too long for the benefit of black type in sales catalogues and to the detriment of racing as an entertainment.

REG GRIFFIN, *Timeform* Dinner, **1987**.

2
Royalty

Dearest Bertie,

Now that Ascot Races are approaching, I wish to repeat *earnestly and seriously*, and with reference to my letters this spring, that I trust you will . . . as my Uncle William IV and Aunt, and we ourselves did, *confine* your *visits* to the Races to the *two* days, *Tuesday* and *Thursday* and not go on *Wednesday* and *Friday*, to which William IV never went, nor did we . . . your example can do *much* for good and do a great deal for evil . . . I hear every true and attached friend of ours expressing *such anxiety* that you should gather round you the really good, steady, and distinguished people.

Letter from QUEEN VICTORIA to Prince of Wales (later Edward VII), in *The Fast Set*.

I fear, Mama, that no year goes round without your giving me a jobation on the subject of racing. . . . The Tuesday and Thursday at Ascot have always been looked upon as the great days as there is the procession in your carriages up the course, which pleases the public and is looked upon by them as a kind of annual pageant. The other days are, of course, of minor importance, but when you have guests staying in your house they naturally like going on those days also, and it would, I think, look both odd and uncivil if I remained at home, and would excite comment if I suddenly deviated from the course I have hitherto adopted. . . . I am always anxious to meet your wishes, dear Mama, in every respect, and I always regret if we are not quite *d'accord* – but as I am past twenty-eight and have some considerable knowledge of the world and society, you will, I am sure, at least I trust, allow me to use my discretion in matters of this kind.

Reply from the PRINCE OF WALES to Queen Victoria.

How fast, how very fast.

QUEEN VICTORIA on seeing Daisy when Lady Brooke (later Countess of Warwick) leaving Windsor Castle in the early hours dressed in hunting pink, in *The Fast Set*.

I am not at all an admirer or approver of our very dull Sundays for I think the absence of innocent amusement for the poor people is mistaken and an encouragement of vice.

QUEEN VICTORIA writing to her daughter, the Princess Royal, in Prussia.

Gazing down [at the first post-war running of The Derby] he saw that the crowd had suddenly parted to let through a long line of disabled men in hospital blue, walking slowly and painfully. The King jerked his hand towards them. 'They have paid the price for us,' he said in his gruff voice. 'Without them there would be no Derby today.'

KENNETH ROSE in *Life of King George V*.

If you can't ride, you know, I'm afraid people will call you a duffer.

KING GEORGE V to the Duke of Windsor, as Prince of Wales.

What do we, as a nation, care about books? How much do you think we spend altogether on our libraries, public or private, as compared with what we spend on horses?

THE QUEEN MOTHER, quoting Ruskin in *Kings & Queens & Courtiers*.

She is the perfect grandmother. She drinks gin, goes racing and is accessible to all. I think she's wonderful. I've come down from Derby to see her. I'd love to paint her portrait. I'm doing Edwina Currie at the moment.

TIMOTHY MORGAN-OWEN, artist, on the Queen Mother.

If it were not for my Archbishop of Canterbury, I should be off in my plane to Longchamps every Sunday.

Attributed to the Queen and related in *Kings & Queens & Courtiers*.

It was quiet in the Royal box. It was as if the affectionate cheers for Devon Loch, which had died a long time ago in a million throats all over Britain, had cast a shadow of silence. There was, after all, very little to be said. Their Majesties tried to comfort me, and said what a beautiful race Devon Loch had run; and in my turn I tried to say how desperately sorry I was that we had not managed to cover those last vital fifty yards.

DICK FRANCIS's description of the scene in the Royal Box at Aintree after Devon Loch's collapse in **1956**.

THE QUEEN: How are you feeling?
CAPTAIN MOORE: Well, Ma'am, I feel like a rabbit who has been bolted by a ferret.
THE QUEEN: I may have been called many things behind my back, but I have never been called a ferret to my face before!

Conversation with her racing manager, whom she was visiting in hospital, **1963**, in *All The Queen's Horses*.

'We're a great pair, Your Majesty. I'm deaf and he's half blind.'

EPH SMITH in the paddock to the Queen.

'Does Linwell like sugar?' the Queen asks me. 'He does not,' I say. 'Does he like carrots, then?' the Queen says. 'He does not,' I say. 'What does he like then, Mallon?' the Queen asks. 'He likes watercress, madam,' I tell her, and she says: 'Oh, does he really, because I'm very partial to watercress myself.'

IVOR HERBERT in *The Queen Mother's Horses*.

The Queen said what tremendous fun this kind of all-in wrestling was. 'Do you want a Royal Charter for them?' I asked, and she said 'No, not yet.'

The Crossman Diaries, **1968**, the year the Jockey Club asked for a Royal Charter. It was granted in 1970.

There are always people around waiting for me to put my foot in it, just like my father.

PRINCESS ANNE.

So the Queen's first pick from her pile of morning newspapers is *The Sporting Life*. Oh well, there's nothing like taking in the facts before going on to the forecasts, fiction and fairy stories in other papers of diverse political persuasions.

NICK O'LINCOLN, *The Racing Specialist.*

I consider it a great honour to ride for the Queen Mother and for Mr Cazalet. I respect the Queen Mother very much. She's so natural. So easy to talk to. She knows all the ins-and-outs of racing. It's fabulous to ride for a woman who really knows the business.

RICHARD DENNARD.

Princess Anne went back to Benenden and still refused to wear the crash hat in the pageant. She was absolutely not going to wear a crash hat and she would ring up Mummy. Well, she rang up Mummy – and she was properly told off. If she was required to wear a crash hat she would jolly well have to do so. And that was the end of it. Princess Anne wore the crash hat.

MRS CHERRIE HATTON-HALL.

When I appear in public people expect me to neigh, grind my teeth, paw the ground and swish my tail.

PRINCESS ANNE.

If the Queen would rather go to Ascot than peer at a lot of dirty nappies in the Institute of Contemporary Arts, what is wrong with that?

Daily Telegraph leader, **1977**.

If you're really involved with horses and want to be successful with them – you know, not just play at it – they don't leave you much time for anything else.

PRINCESS ANNE, interviewed by Kenneth Harris, the *Observer*.

My own ambition is to get a Derby winner for the Queen and breed one for myself as well. I hope they don't come in the same year.

THE EARL OF CARNARVON, the Queen's racing manager, **1983**.

Ma'am, if you'd never won a race,
The Turf would still be blessed in you
Who, with the worst of luck to face,
Still come serenely smiling through.
And that is why in happier hours
When you stand in the winner's place
We treat your wins, like you, as ours.

JOHN BLISS, after the Queen Mother's 200th winner in **1969**, *The Sporting Life.*

Racing just seemed like a natural extension of my riding. It began because I was taking part in a charity race and I found that I enjoyed riding out first thing in the morning. It was only when I got into the paddock I thought, 'What the heck are you doing here? This is madness.'

THE PRINCESS ROYAL, *Woman's Own*, **1987**.

It's one of the real sports that's left to us: a bit of danger and a bit of excitement, and the horses, which are the best thing in the world.

THE QUEEN MOTHER.

David Nicholson asked me if I could find the Princess Royal a suitable mount a year ago but he only let her come and ride out once. I expect he didn't want her to pick up our bad Newmarket habits.

MICHAEL STOUTE, quoted after the win by the Princess Royal on Ten No Trumps, **1987**.

Among the massive crowds for Diamond Day at Ascot on Saturday, one urgent voice in the stands exhorted: 'Don't be so cool, do something.' This self-confessed plea came not from an ordinary punter, but from the Queen as she shouted home the Princess Royal in the Dresden Diamond Stakes.

TONY STAFFORD, *Daily Telegraph*, **1987**.

3
Owners

Hermit's Derby broke my heart. But I didn't show it, did I?

LORD HASTINGS (**1842–1868**).

Before you are a year older you may hear of an Owners' Association for the protection of the unfortunate creature who is fool enough not to race for his own money, pay for the stabling of his horses at race meetings and many other abuses, but *this is private.*

LORD WOLVERTON writing to his trainer, **1904**.

Leopold de Rothschild, after Danny Maher had ridden a winner for him:
   'With all due deference to you, Maher, the best jockey I have seen in my life – you included – is Fordham.'
   Maher: 'So I have always heard, Sir'.

From *The Fast Set.*

I have had many good friends in my life and known many delightful men, but the most perfect gentleman of all was Lord Derby.

GEORGE LAMBTON on the 17th Earl, **1924**.

I do not own and do not wish to own a stud of thoroughbreds or a racing stable. So many people I know own racehorses as a matter of snobbishness. They cannot even recognize their own horses when they see them.

NUBAR GULBENKIAN.

He is dead lazy, so in case the influence of Morpheus overcomes him during the course of the contest, tie a bootlace on the end of your shillelagh before you put to sea, and fetch him a couple round his streptococci when you have gone half way.

BERT RICH, giving orders to his jockey.

I am getting to be so big they are calling me the Aga Cohen.

BUD FLANAGAN, comedian.

Wouldn't it be enough to turn any girl's head coming down to breakfast one morning on her twenty-first birthday, and opening a letter containing a cheque for a million pounds from her solicitor, and the promise that there was plenty more to come?

OWEN ANTHONY on Dorothy Paget.

Much of Dorothy Paget's kindness was unadvertised. How many people of the Turf, I wonder, knew of her visits to Wormwood Scrubs to sing to the prisoners?

But her kindness, like the rest of her ways, was capricious. After Golden Miller had won the Grand National in 1934, for example, she gave trainer, jockey and head lad (among other gifts) a 3-foot statuette of the horse – in chocolate.

From *Golden Miller*.

Too much money . . . too soon. An appropriate epitaph for the Hon. Dorothy Wyndham Paget. Dead at the age of fifty-four, forty-three of her years had been spent in pleasing herself. She became a millionairess at the age of eleven . . . that was her tragedy. Poor little rich girl! That phrase might have been written for her.

Her glory? Mostly reflected. She chose the Turf as her playground and, by chance, became associated with Golden Miller, one of the greatest horses of all time. . . . We shall remember her as the bulky, Glastonbury-booted figure which appeared on the racecourse surrounded by a retinue of servants. We shall reminisce about her bad manners, enormous appetite and extraordinary clothes.

And we shall miss her!

LEN SCOTT, *The Sporting Life*, **1960**.

Murless's owners were basically the old type of owner-breeder who did everything by the book and they didn't give the extra presents which the modern man was coming along and giving.

They were often very mean because the English aristocracy is notoriously mean and they didn't understand that you've got to give these guys extra encouragement because there are all sorts of bookmakers and others willing to give them God knows what to lose, so you've got to make it a bit better than the standard ten per cent.

RICHARD BAERLEIN, quoted in *Lester* by Sean Pryor.

In 1959 I had a little two-year-old which had cost £400. It was an election year and I wanted to name it Vote Labour. The Jockey Club refused permission, disapproving of political propaganda paraded on the racecourse.

WOODROW WYATT in *To The Pack*.

You now see before you the spectacle of a once proud sport reduced to utter dependence on public money.

SIR DAVID ROBINSON, Gimcrack Dinner speech, **1969**.

I am in favour of a means test for owners.

DUKE OF DEVONSHIRE, Gimcrack Dinner, **1969**.

I think the late Aga Khan, who had derived immense benefits from English racing, did the sport lamentable disservice by letting his stallions go overseas. It would have been a different and a happier story if Blenheim, Bahram, Mahmoud and Nasrullah had stayed in this country or in Ireland.

SIR JACK JARVIS, *British Racehorse*, **1969**.

We must be strong enough if necessary to make the Treasury moderate its tax demands and even to strike if there is no other way of securing fair treatment.

JOHN BAILLIE, president of the Racehorse Owners Association, **1970**.

In two years all owners will be millionaires – the Jockey Club will

see to that. Why do they refuse to let our moderate horses have
races for themselves and then turn round and award a £2000 race
for Newmarket-trained horses only?

JOE HARTIGAN.

It is not enough to say racing is a sport. We must all show
sportsmanship.

SIR DAVID ROBINSON.

I won't be happy until a horse owned by a working men's club
wins the Derby.

LORD WIGG.

Let's not be complicated. You want to know how much I enjoy
my racing. The answer is that I enjoy it tremendously when things
go well but that I worry terribly when things go wrong or if
accidents occur. My racehorses are my whole life.

LADY BEAVERBROOK, *Financial Times*.

Owners and trainers are being spoon fed. They must realize that
they owe something to racing, particularly as punters – through
the levy – are providing so much prize money.

SIR STANLEY RAYMOND, chairman of the Betting and Gaming Board, in the *Daily
Mail*, **1973**.

Lord Sefton also experienced the wry wit of Syd Mercer when
observing that his horse, narrowly beaten by Syd's Pillow Fight
at Birmingham, really deserved to have been first past the post.
    'You definitely should have won, my lord, but the Lord
Almighty knew where it was needed most,' replied Syd.

SYD MERCER talking to Colin Fleetwood-Jones in *Pacemaker*, **1974**.

Owning racehorses is a rich man's sport. Nobody makes him do
it. There are no poor owners. I say again, there are no poor
owners.

LORD LEVERHULME, senior steward, **1974**.

George Wigg, who had bought a sky blue cap from an Indian groom for 9d., said his colours would be khaki shirt and sky blue cap. Colonel Bell, having recovered from his shock that an NCO should be the owner, bellowed, 'There's no such colour as khaki! It was invented by the War Office during the South African war.'

TIM FITZGEORGE-PARKER, 1974.

Kelly's Hero carried the bizarre colours of John Mulhern . . . red jacket with large white question mark back and front. A friend observes: 'If the jockey does not know if he's trying, what chance have we got.'

JONATHAN POWELL at Galway races, 1974.

Don't make me out as a total philanthropist – it's for my own conscience.

CHARLES ST GEORGE on the insurance he provides for jockeys who ride for him.

Owners are the key, and I speak as an owner myself. If trainers cannot pay their staff properly without increasing fees to owners, then they must increase fees. Owners who cannot afford the increase must get out. Nobody forces us to own horses. It's a pleasure.

NOEL WHITCOMB, 1975.

I am attracted to the Turf because you meet a lot of high-class people in racing.

NELSON BUNKER HUNT.

We have been involved in racing so long, it is astonishing we were not born with hooves.

DANIEL WILDENSTEIN, 1977.

They'll pretty soon leave you if you're not successful, no matter who you are.

WILLIAM HASTINGS-BASS on owners, 1977.

I suppose I know ten per cent of what there is to know and when I am eighty I might know twenty per cent.

ROBERT SANGSTER, 1977.

In the final analysis no one really knows which horse is going to win, certainly not the owner.

ROBERT MORLEY, 1977.

I would have liked to have celebrated, only I had a horse running the next day and had to get to bed early.

SIR HUMPHREY DE TRAFFORD telling Robert Morley why he retired to bed at seven o'clock with two boiled eggs the night he won the Derby, *Pacemaker*, 1977.

Even when you have risen at some unearthly hour, driven countless miles to Wolverhampton and arrived in time to see your horse finish eighth in a field of eight in a race he should have won, there is always hope and a curious feeling of having come very near to making a fortune.

ROBERT MORLEY.

There is little to compare with the thrill of standing next to the creature in the winner's enclosure avoiding his hooves and receiving the congratulations of the press, your trainer and the friends who backed it. What makes the experience so satisfying is that you yourself have had absolutely nothing to do with the horse winning.

ROBERT MORLEY.

I must be one of the unluckiest men in racing. You know all the racing stories of bad luck? Well I could tell the lot and double them.

VICTOR (now Lord) MATTHEWS, 1978.

My grandfather once told me: 'You can judge a man by his bookcase and his boots.'

VICTOR MATTHEWS.

At his insistence, a leading jockey was offered the ride for £1000 and accepted. The jockey, on entering the paddock, was horrified to find Garfield Weston trying to hand the retainer over to him in bank notes. 'Not now,' the worried jockey exclaimed, 'the television cameras are on us.'

'Setting The Pace,' *Pacemaker*, **1978**.

Partnerships can be difficult. One partner may be too canny. Another may want too much control.

ROBERT SANGSTER, **1979**.

There is nothing in the world that could move the horse. People have wanted to buy shares, a piece of the action. But for me and Audrey this isn't about money or investment. This is about some joy in our lives. It's faith. And it's love too.

MAX MUINOS, owner of Ela-Mana-Mou, on being asked what he would do if he was offered £1m for the horse.

Lord Howard de Walden takes the view that one million is pretty much like another.

PETER O'SULLEVAN.

It is vulgar to win the Derby two years running.

LORD WEINSTOCK.

I was surprised to read in your papers that Mr Robert Sangster is regarded over here as a rich man.

A visiting sheikh, *The Racehorse*, **1980**.

I don't like selling my racehorses. They're my pets.

LORD WEINSTOCK.

It's the one criticism I have of the racing game. It's a very jealous industry.

ROBERT SANGSTER.

Every owner is saying, 'Please don't send me up to Edinburgh,' but I think that it's much less tiring to go up to Edinburgh with a chance than to go down the road where you know you haven't got a hope.

SIR MARK PRESCOTT, **1981**.

Poor chap, they were all after him and he died at forty-eight, a victim of wine and women.

SAM ARMSTRONG on the Maharajah of Baroda, **1981**.

I met the Maharajah of Baroda at Poole in Dorset when he arrived by flying-boat accompanied by his doctor and his Australian jockey, Edgar Britt. All three wore uniforms. The Maharajah was dressed as a general and Britt as a captain in the Baroda Lancers. When I said to a friend that I didn't like the look of them, he told me never to judge a sausage by its skin.

SAM ARMSTRONG, as above.

I'm not having that old bugger coming here on a Sunday. I won't see people on Sunday.

REG HOBBS, father of Bruce, on one of his owners, Lord Bicester, who unsurprisingly later removed his horses, *Pacemaker*, **1981**.

Another fairly typical pre-war owner was Sir William Nelson whose carmine complexion suggested that his reputation as a connoisseur of old brandy was not misplaced. He had made a stack of money importing frozen meat from the Argentine and he was reportedly not all that pleased when Robin Goodfellow of the *Daily Mail* rather cheekily described him as 'a dead meat merchant', the remark being thought to contain an innuendo in respect of Sir William's horses.

ROGER MORTIMER, **1982**.

Just before the great battle of Arras, Jim Joel wrote to his father and said he was short of a charger. His fond papa, knowing less about war than finance, sent him out a horse that had been placed in the Middle Park Stakes.

ROGER MORTIMER on Jim Joel's experience as an officer in the First World War, *Pacemaker*, **1982**.

Everything has its price – there is no horse born that is priceless.

SHEIKH MOHAMMED, **1982**.

Of course, I want my horse to win, but if he can't then I want my brother's to come first.

SHEIKH MOHAMMED.

When you've followed a bird across the desert with your falcon, and they are chasing in the air, it's my bird against him, a 50–50 chance. For me, it's the same thing as an exciting race between horses.

SHEIKH MOHAMMED.

I've never been keen on owners being subsidized. No one puts a gun at people's heads forcing them to own a racehorse. It's a rich person's hobby so why should it be subsidized? No one subsidizes your hobbies, do they? This is based on greed. Just watch all the Rolls-Royces line up at Newmarket. Their owners are not exactly caught in the poverty trap.

MRS JOHN HISLOP.

The whole thing has become stupidly expensive. I wouldn't dream of getting involved in the Keeneland nonsense. They still breed the best horses in the world in Britain and Ireland. So I shall continue to buy British and I shall continue to buy at Tattersalls.

MR RAVI TIKKOO.

He was a stickler for detail. He had a canteen at the back of the yard for the lads and he said to me, 'Bill, go and check up on that canteen. They're overcharging me. Three eggs missing last week.'

LORD HARRINGTON on the late owner David Robinson, **1984**.

The Arabs operate as they do with their falcon trainers: he is the key man and whatever he says is allowed to go. Their trust in trainers is huge.

NICK CLARKE, *Pacemaker*, **1985**.

We don't want to throw our weight around, and we don't try to alter your conventions. We enjoy our horses. We don't bet. We run them all honestly and fairly and we thoroughly enjoy British racing.

SHEIKH MOHAMMED, **1985**.

There were plenty of knives put in the back of Daniel Wildenstein when he decided to remove his horses from Warren Place, but you won't hear many complaints about the French art dealer from Henry Cecil's stable lads. When the horses left Cecil after Royal Ascot, Wildenstein showed there is another side to this man, painted so black by some hacks. For he repaid the kindness shown by the lads by giving them £500 for each of his horses they looked after. And that meant a £1000 gift for the lad who put Vertige and Grand Pavois through their paces. Now who's a bad fella?

The *Weekender*, **1985**.

The owners you don't get on with are the ones who pay you the money to do a job and then want to do it themselves.

MICK RYAN, **1985**.

Because of three Bedouin princes, some misapplied American tax dodges, and a Mersey bookmaker's horse-dealing son, the world's finest horses are suddenly again training and running on English grass.

NORMAN MACRAE, commenting on the extraordinary growth in importation into this country of US thoroughbreds in *The Economist*, **1985**.

You never see a pretty unattached girl on a racecourse. But you often see positive gangs of rather unpretty ones. They are the owners or owners' wives and they wear mink in all weathers and far too much make-up. For some odd reason, I can never work out why they always seem to be married to haulage contractors in the North, builders in the South and farmers in the West.

JEFFREY BERNARD.

My ambition in life isn't to be held up outside Stringfellow's by Samantha Fox.

TERRY RAMSDEN.

If a horse can't run I won't sell it for dogmeat.

TERRY RAMSDEN.

I don't necessarily think that pure money buys what you want –
as you see when you find $10 million colts who aren't fit to pull
a Whitbread's cart.

TERRY RAMSDEN.

I don't care whether I'm talking to Robert Sangster or Joe Smith
from Streatham.

TERRY RAMSDEN.

I never did think that Shady Heights could win the Derby. It's
owned by some bloke from Hong Kong. People like that don't
win the Derby.

Chester racegoer quoted by CHRISTOPHER POOLE, **1987**.

Owners are no different from anyone else in that they don't like
to be seen to have made fools of themselves. If you've got a good
horse, and something goes wrong, it sours you. I mean it can sour
an owner. I know it sounds silly but it's true.

LOUIS FREEDMAN, **1987**.

What, you wonder, was a racehorse-owning property dealer and
estate agent doing serving on the Race Relations Board? He
smiles the beatific smile, but there is sharpness in his reply. 'Had
it occurred to you,' he asks with just a bit of self-mockery thrown
in to counter any charges of pomposity, 'that I might be interested
in the dignity of mankind?'

PAUL HAIGH – LOUIS FREEDMAN in conversation, **1987**.

He always takes the piss, and even tells me how to ride his horses!
I answer him back and we get on well. If you do, you get a clash
of characters. He digs and digs and digs to try to get you annoyed.
Anyone who is annoyed always tells the truth – but I don't fall
for his style.

WILLIE CARSON on Lord Weinstock.

Wot, float in a yacht all day drinking cocktails and chasing blondes? Not me, mate. I suppose if I wanted to be a playboy, I could. But life's too short. There's too many things to do. Next time I might come back as a pussy cat.

TERRY RAMSDEN.

Robinson's approach to racing was highly professional. He graded his horses for courses and ran his string like a business at a time when such an approach was not the done thing. This did not endear him to the Jockey Club and he in turn regarded them as amateurs.

Obituary to Sir David Robinson, *The Times*, **1987**.

The man who wins is the one who walks away with a profit.

TERRY RAMSDEN, **1987**.

It is hard to find any pity for a man whose financial resources were estimated in 1980 to be $8 billion and whose downfall has come about largely because of his disastrous attempt to corner the world's silver market. Any spare sympathy should instead be directed towards some of the old horses who have served Hunt so well over the years and who now face the indignity of being traipsed through the sales ring.

JOHN COBB, on the dispersal of all Nelson Bunker Hunt's 596 racehorses, the *Independent*.

The trainer approached the owner and said, 'I'm afraid he's still green,' and the owner replied, 'He was brown the last time I saw him.'

HENRY CECIL illustrating the ignorance of some owners, *Racing World*, **1988**.

4

Jockeys

A jockey's evidence is nearly always useless. He is not riding as a witness and is likely to be biased one way or another. Sometimes this is caused by sheer bad temper after an irritating incident, sometimes memory failure, sometimes a policy of 'I'll scratch your back'.

On the other hand if your inquiry board has any weak links in it, a steward, for instance, who is wrong in what he says, or speaks in a hectoring manner, an experienced rider will be quick to make him look a fool; and rightly so.

KENNETH STEWART in *Racing Control.*

If a horse is to be punished at all, he should be hit hard, well below the stifle and, preferably, left-handed. If he is merely looking around him, a smart tap on the shoulder, without taking the hand off the rein, should be sufficient to remind him that he is not there for sightseeing and be unlikely to cause a dissolution of the partnership.

In the case of a well-trained, manageable horse, therefore, the use of the whip is confined to encouragement and guidance. The damage done by improper use of the whip on the racecourse cannot be overestimated.

JOHN HISLOP in *Flat Race Riding.*

It amazes me how well the majority of jump jockeys ride in a race until they've landed over the last, then how badly most of them ride a finish. Apart from a half-dozen, they look like coster boys sitting on top of donkeys' behinds, bashing about with shillelaghs.

JACK LEACH in *A Rider on the Stand.*

Taking what the Fates provide them
Danger calling. Death beside them
'Tis a game beyond gain saying
Made by Gods for brave men's playing.

WILL OGILVY.

Jockeys may not like what I say but they are servants, and well paid ones, and when they sit up all night in the middle of a race week, they are grossly neglecting their duties to their employers.

GEORGE LAMBTON in *Men and Horses I Have Known*.

'Harry had the Captain in the same position as a man with a cork halfway in the neck of a bottle; one little push and it will go down!'

CHARLES GREENWOOD, *Daily Telegraph*, on a finish between Harry Beasley and Roddy Owen.

'My lords, dukes and gentlemen! If I rides and wins they says I rides foul. If I rides and only gets a place they says there's something fishy.

If I rides and am among the also rans they says I'm not trying and if there's bumping and boring it's me they picks on as guilty.

I have a good wife at home, some money in the bank, and I doesn't care a damn what you does with me. I always rides straight and rides to win and I'm fed up.'

'SPEEDY' PAYNE, up before stewards in Yorkshire. He left the stewards' room without even a caution.

Gallop 'em for brass. They gallop for nowt at home and that is no bloody good to anybody.

JACK LEACH in *A Rider on the Stand*.

Never drop your anchor in the harbour, drop it out at sea.

Old-timer's advice in *The Wit of The Turf*.

I see no particular objection to giving women a chance to ride in races now and again . . . such races should be on the Flat and be placed last on the card so that those racegoers not interested can return home for tea and 'Magic Roundabout'.

ROGER MORTIMER.

Freud put up the equivalent over weight of twenty-two one-pound tins of dog food.

PETER O'SULLEVAN, on the pilot of Winter Fair riding in a match against Sir Hugh Fraser aboard Star Award.

I can tell everything I want to know about a man by the way he sits on a horse.

LORD LONSDALE in *The Yellow Earl*.

It is becoming increasingly obvious that Flat race jockeys with their statutory ten per cent of winning stake money and probably handsome presents in cash or kind on top are being overpaid.

CLIVE GRAHAM.

Collectively we seem to lack the pluck to say boo to a jockey. Of course, there are well-known excuses for this feeble attitude, but I doubt if they are really valid. Unfortunately, immunity of criticism gives certain jockeys a ludicrously exaggerated view of their own skill and importance.

ROGER MORTIMER, *The Racehorse*.

Dennis McKay, who loses his apprentice allowance next season on reaching his twenty-third year, should still have plenty of opportunities in handicap races – even if, due to his size and youthful appearance, he is still apt to get a quizzical look from the barmaid when ordering half-a-pint of shandy.

CLIVE GRAHAM, *Daily Express*, **1969**.

Not many jockeys are racing bred. They come from the big cities, the slums. They come from the Gorbals or the Liverpool Docks, and a lot come over from Ireland, and that is why they love it, because it's an escape. They may not make high wages but they live well enough, and they like the horses, and they aren't cooped up in slums.

FRANK CUNDELL, *Daily Telegraph* magazine.

It's hell dancing with jockeys. It's 'Ouch, don't put your hand there' and 'Mind my bad shoulder' all the time – and it's the same in bed, I may say.

A lady quoted in the *Observer*.

Somehow I can't see women riding under Jockey Club rules. They are not the right shape, for one thing.

MISS NORAH WILMOT, on Mrs Goodhew's application for a licence to ride over hurdles, *Daily Mail*.

A woman's place is at home warming her husband's slippers.

COLONEL FRANK WELDON.

In the early days, you went to a trainer and you 'yes-sir'd him. Now, the trainers 'yes-sir' you!

RICHARD 'BONES' INGERSOLL, American jockey's agent, **1974**.

I've only known three cases in my time where a race was reckoned to be fixed, but each time the wrong horse won.

ERNIE HALES, master valet.

It's funny that a lot of people when they finish racing, like Charlie Smirke and Harry Carr, never go again.

TOM E. WEBSTER, **1975**.

After the three-year-old hurdle, one experienced jockey said to me: 'There was one fellow whose horse had no chance, yet he was hitting him as I went past and I could hear the blows still falling as I went away. That can't be right.' It isn't. It comes from ignorance, and in some cases just raw, harsh brutality, and a really strong lead from the stewards is needed to stamp it out. Don't expect this column to stay silent.

BROUGH SCOTT, *Sunday Times*.

It's a pity to get rid of traditions that don't do any harm. If a famous jockey becomes a Sir, it makes him happy without making me unhappy.

WILLIAM DOUGLAS HOME, *Observer* magazine.

There they were, getting trodden on, then getting up only to be knocked down again. Remarkable. I could only think they were either mad or just absolutely fearless. Now I know that most of the time it's the latter.

GERRY CRANHAM, photographer, 1977.

It was to my amazement and dismay that the Racing Calendar has announced the new conditions for the claiming jump jockey's licence. We are going back thirty or forty years to ask young jockeys to ride for half fees. This unfair practice was stopped years ago and now has reappeared for God knows what reason. If a boy is given the chance to ride, he is entitled to a full fee. There is no earthly reason why a trainer should receive half his fees.

BOB TURNELL, 1978.

Yes, they tried to con me at the gate, and pride aside, they succeeded sometimes.

ALEC MARSH, senior starter, on the old-style starting gates, 1978.

If there is a chance of a ride, the young jockey must bloody well go and ride it.

DAVID NICHOLSON, 1979.

No sex before a race? That's a load of cobblers. No one who knows jockeys could imagine them saying, 'Not tonight, darling. I am riding in the National tomorrow.'

JENNY PITMAN.

You hear and read an awful lot about boys not getting the chance to ride, but how many have really got the ambition when you get down to it?

GUY HARWOOD, 1979.

What's the matter with the British? Why don't you shout? In America we all shout at all sports, and it makes the sportsmen perform better. They are artistes. My husband is an artiste. I shout, 'Come on come on,' but you are quiet. What is the matter?

MRS ANGEL CORDERO, wife of one of America's leading jockeys, **1980**.

Either you were out on the tiles all night, or you stopped the horse and did me. Which was it?

FRED RIMELL to a losing jockey, **1981**.

If a man goes round telling his jockeys to give his horses easy races all over the place, it's not surprising if the jockeys will sometimes show a bit of private enterprise.

TOM JONES, **1981**.

You must remember we have these athletes called jockeys who are known throughout the world and people want to see these highly skilled men just as much as good horses.

MIKE WATT, former agent to Lester Piggott, **1981**.

I would take the boys at the age of twelve, judging by their height, weight, knees and hands and lightness of bone whether they were liable to put on weight. I liked them to weigh no more than 4st 7lb at the age of fourteen.

SAM ARMSTRONG on picking apprentice jockeys, **1981**.

People always ask me how many races over here are fixed – jockeys' races if you like. I don't know but perhaps in the region of twenty a year.

PETER SMILES, director of Racing Security Services, **1981**.

The one who wins most races for me.

SHEIKH MOHAMMED nominates his favourite jockey, **1982**.

Jockeys were locked up in the racecourse hostel at declaration time on Friday and were not released until after their last ride on Sunday.

BROUGH SCOTT on racing in Japan, **1983**.

If jockeys haven't some devilment in them they will never reach the top.

RYAN PRICE, talking to Richard Baerlein, in *Owners*.

I'm not a bit interested in Flat racing and it's none of my business. But I've watched some of the races on television and I'm amazed. If a horse decides to swerve, there's nothing any jockey can do about it for even a fraction of a second. And that's when the trouble occurs. Common sense seems to have gone out of the window when some of these cases have been dealt with.

FRED WINTER, *The Times*.

I think that French jump jockeys are better riders.

ANDRÉ FABRE, French trainer, **1983**.

Of course jockeys bet. They don't put it on themselves. They get friends or relations to do it.

ERIC MOLLER, owner, **1984**.

If a jockey has helped make a horse and it is then syndicated for over half a million pounds, he's entitled to 2½ per cent.

ROBERT SANGSTER, *Sunday Express* magazine, **1984**.

I take issue with the people who see the last few furlongs of a race and say that Piggott or Francome gave up a long way out, without having seen they've been hard at work for a mile.

JOHN SHARRATT, race-reader, **1985**.

I don't think people fully realize how badly off we are going to be in the next few years when we lose both Piggott and Francome.

JOHN SHARRATT.

Everyone in racing from the head of RSS down to the humblest bookie's floorman knows that jockeys have their 'punters'.

'Saturday Opinion', *The Sporting Life*, **1986**.

All the jockeys would have grumbled about being barked at and called by their surnames but they would have gone on putting up with it if it hadn't been for that Yorkshire TV programme on the Jockey Club.

GEOFFREY SUMMERS, ex-secretary to the Jockeys' Association, **1986**.

I think that the doper in this country has a very hard time and would be better off going somewhere else.

GEOFFREY SUMMERS.

I believe jockeys are the last people in racing entitled to draw anything from the money made by the new satellite television in betting shops. Yes, I do think they are being greedy in pressing for such a claim.

MAURICE CAMACHO.

Noel Coward's advice to actors about to take the stage was: 'Blow your nose and check your flies.' More serious instructions to a jockey might be to acquaint himself with the course and not to forget to weigh in.

DAVID HADERT, the *Guardian*.

It's bad enough us racing hacks banging on about how tough a time Eddery and Cauthen have in earning their millions, but this past week we have also had the soccer ace Steve Hodge feeling homesick in London, and the cricketer Javed Miandad mouthing oaths at everyone in Rawalpindi.

Of course sport is tough, but so too is lavatory-cleaning, and there are no star salaries in the latrines. It's sad if young Steve misses his mates in the Midlands, or if stroppy Javed meets an umpire with guts to give him out lbw in front of a Pakistani crowd, but both get paid, and handsomely.

So let's end with someone who never complained through the most dreadful of injuries, whose whole sporting life has been a truth, and who in his early days was caught up in a hurricane almost as fierce as Friday's. It was at Newcastle one November, and Jonjo O'Neill got unseated in the novice 'chase. The disbelieving trainer began to grumble. 'But I couldn't help it sir,' stuttered our youthful hero. 'I was blown off.'

BROUGH SCOTT, *Sunday Times*.

Frenchie Nicholson once claimed that on one particularly foggy afternoon at Wincanton in the late forties he took a horse out into the centre during the three-mile hurdle and joined in a circuit later.

'Gosh,' I said. 'How far did you win by?'

'Ah no,' he replied with that famous boyish twinkle in his eye, 'he didn't win. But he finished so well everyone kept asking if he was for sale.'

BROUGH SCOTT, *Sunday Times*.

To a jockey £50 for excessive use of the whip is absurd. Either he is guilty of an obnoxious offence which the Jockey Club are trying to stamp out, in which case he deserves a severe punishment, or he is innocent. Fining a jockey £50 for such an offence is akin to fining a motorist 20p for exceeding the speed limit.

RICHARD BAERLEIN, the *Guardian*, **1988**.

Fred Archer

Backers have lost the best friend they ever had.

LORD MARCUS BERESFORD on the death of Fred Archer.

It's a great mistake to knock a horse about, and I know that a few years back I was a severe rider, but I've learnt by experience. I rarely hit a horse more than twice in a finish and I rarely or never have rowels to my spurs.

FRED ARCHER.

Gee Armytage

I know that I'm never going to be as strong as most male jockeys, but what I lack in strength, and maybe natural talent, I think I make up for in really wanting to win.

GEE ARMYTAGE, **1988**.

Cash Asmussen

The pace is different here. I believe that a lot of races in France – not so many in England – are run at a false pace and I think we've changed that a bit.

CASH ASMUSSEN, **1983**.

He's got no bloody idea. Where 'av they found 'im from?

Chester racegoer on Cash Asmussen, quoted by Christopher Poole, **1987**.

I came in with a big profile, with big shoes to fill. I'm a big boy. I can take it.

CASH ASMUSSEN.

Mary Bacon

Mary and her husband rode in opposition to each other for a while. When Johnny Bacon finished second to Mary one day, he became annoyed with the teasing he received. The next time they rode in the same race, Johnny tried to knock Mary's horse off stride. Hardly a demure young thing, Mary took the next opportunity she got to try and put her husband over the fence in a race. The stewards suspended Mary for five days.

'Okay, I got five days,' she says she told her husband. 'You get five nights.'

JANE GOLDSTEIN on American jockey, Mary Bacon, **1974**.

Ron Barry

A couple of lengths covered the field for the first half-mile and I thought the proceedings needed livening up a bit. So I started a chorus of 'Show Me The Way To Go Home'. Somebody else joined in, then another and pretty soon we were all on a top note.

RON BARRY describing a jockeys' chorus at Ayr, **1984**.

I wanted to go out on a winner rather than on a stretcher.

RON BARRY on why he retired after riding the aptly named Final Argument to victory at Ayr, **1984**.

Paul Barton

I told a West country trainer that his horse, which had tailed off in a novice chase, would be nice when he matured. 'How much time does he need?' he asked me. 'He's already eleven.'

PAUL BARTON, quoted by Marcus Armytage, *Horse and Hound*.

Mark Birch

I rode Sea Pigeon in all his work – that's why my arms are so long.

MARK BIRCH, **1983**.

Scobie Breasley

I had a marvellous relationship with Sir Gordon Richards – we never had a cross word in all the time I rode for him. He never gave me any riding instructions – mind you I wouldn't have taken any notice of them anyway!

SCOBIE BREASLEY, **1977**.

John Buckingham

Some people look at me and say, 'Poor old bugger. He won the National and now he's doing the washing.'

JOHN BUCKINGHAM, ex-jockey and master valet, **1978**.

In the afternoon I went up to London to appear on 'Sunday Night at the Palladium'. That was much more frightening than riding in the National.

JOHN BUCKINGHAM.

Harry Carr

The average French jockey, with the best will in the world, just can't stay calm when the pressure is on.

HARRY CARR, Queen's jockey, in *Sportsfan*, **1970**.

Over the years Britain has steadily produced the best jockeys in Europe, quite possibly the best in the world. But unless we devote more time to the apprentices, this flow of talent will dry up very rapidly . . . and we could so very easily become just another horse-riding nation.

HARRY CARR, **1973**.

Willie Carson

I'm not a natural rider. It has taken very hard work to learn the business. The only natural I know is Lester Piggott. I've come late on the scene, but that's not a bad thing. Jockeys who get success too early sometimes blow it.

WILLIE CARSON, *Sunday Mirror*.

The one thing you could say about me as a kid was that I was a good newspaper boy.

WILLIE CARSON, **1977**.

He was so tiny that I used to wonder sometimes how he was going to manage.

MRS MAY CARSON on her son Willie, 1977.

Half-dressed when I arrived, in a bright yellow Japanese kimono, Mr Carson looked like a daffodil. Very fresh for early morning and so small I could have plucked him off the carpet with one hand. The face is boyish. In fact, coltish. Pointed ears. Longish nose. The big square teeth and a brown forelock bumping up and down between his frisky blue eyes.

JEAN ROOK, *Daily Express*.

Willie Carson extracted an out of character and yet honest remark from Cauthen after chastising him, 'Steve had done something stupid and I called him an idiot – or even worse. He replied very coolly, "Yeah, but a rich one." It made me chuckle coming from "The Kid" but put me in my place.'

TIM RICHARDS, *The Field*.

Steve Cauthen

I'm ready to start, Dad. I'm ready to ride.

STEVE CAUTHEN, on his sixteenth birthday.

He's got natural ability. Whatever he's learned, he's learned well. And he's got me.

LENNY GOODMAN, Steve Cauthen's agent, 1978.

The horse is such a beautiful animal. When you're on him, in control of him, moving with him, it is a beautiful feeling.

STEVE CAUTHEN, 1978.

In this game you're only as good as your last ride – just like many think horses are only as good as their last run.

STEVE CAUTHEN, 1981.

Basically, I enjoy riding over and above money and everything else.

STEVE CAUTHEN.

Now you can see why I've backed Steve Cauthen to become champion jockey. He has a right cut and reminds me very much of myself at my best.

PAUL KELLEWAY, *The Times*.

I am still a country kid. Racing is a rough business on the temper. Jockeys yell at each other. Trainers yell at jockeys. Owners get mad with trainers. Jockeys swear – maybe under their breaths – at trainers and owners. And when all that's over for the day I like to come home, open the windows in my cottage at Lambourn, and listen to birdsong.

STEVE CAUTHEN, *Daily Mail*.

In a sense jockeys are like actors and I don't like playing to a dead crowd.

STEVE CAUTHEN, comparing British racegoers favourably to their American counterparts, **1985**.

I think experience, not just strength, has made me a better jockey. Learning to get the most out of a horse, that's the important thing.

STEVE CAUTHEN.

I know dozens who have spilt more alcohol than our champion jockey has swallowed.

MONTY COURT, The *Weekender*, **1985**, dismissing sensational tabloid reports of Steve Cauthen's alleged drink problem.

I was nearly a complete jockey at eighteen but the small gap between what I was then and what I am today took years to fill.

STEVE CAUTHEN.

It's funny. Human nature, I guess. Everybody loves you, then they want you to fall.

STEVEN CAUTHEN, champion jockey.

Bob Champion

As far as I was concerned there was no point in living if I couldn't be a jockey.

BOB CHAMPION, **1981**.

Who can blame him if, at times, there was a scarcely concealed desperation about some of his race riding?

JONATHAN POWELL on cancer-recovering Bob Champion in *Champion's Story*, **1981**.

A girl is a danger to everyone else. I am dead against them. They are simply not strong enough or big enough. It's strength that holds horses together when they tire after jumping and you can't expect women to have that.

BOB CHAMPION, *Daily Mail*.

Nicky Connorton

Bill would put me on a horse which could take a strong hold. 'Go to the back of the string and see how few you can pass,' he'd say. The first morning on the gallops, I passed the lot, but eventually I got the hang of things.

NICKY CONNORTON, jockey, on his apprenticeship with Bill Watts, **1986**.

Paul Cook

If Paul Cook had committed his daring act in a Western he might have got away with it. Had he done so in France he'd have been in the Bastille within an hour and they would have thrown away the key.

PETER O'SULLEVAN on a piece of alleged reckless riding by Cook, *Daily Express*, **1979**.

Angel Cordero Jr

Call him the Great Intimidator. He will beat you with his head, his whip, his hands or his heart. But he *will* beat you.

JAY HOVDEY on American jockey Angel Cordero Jr, **1985**.

Tony Cruz

It is a real partnership. I am the boss in the morning. He is the boss in the afternoon.

PATRICK BIANCONE on his jockey Tony Cruz, **1987**.

Here they start off slow and then just get faster and faster. Here you get time to think. Maybe the horse gets too much time to think if you're not careful.

TONY CRUZ on riding in France, **1987**.

Hywel Davies

The longer a young rider goes on without a winner, the better. Too much success early on and they begin to think their job's easy.

HYWEL DAVIES, *Newbury Weekly News*.

Eddie Dempsey

Eddie stood beside the tombstone last week. He was asked what he was thinking, what nostalgic sentiments were running through his head. 'I was just wondering,' he said, 'if any man ever had a hangover like the one this little horse gave me.'

EDDIE DEMPSEY, **1979**.

Richard Dennard

'I don't want to finish up on the bread line.' Many jump jockeys, he claims, are almost down to that level. So much so, in fact, that they have had to take food from the tracks home to feed their family. 'We have a table of sandwiches and biscuits in our changing rooms and I have seen some jockeys filling their bags so they can give something to their children.'

RICHARD DENNARD, *Evening News*, **1973**.

Dave Dick

Dave Dick had travelled up to Sedgefield with Arthur Freeman. In the dressing room, Freeman was injudicious enough to remark to Dick that they had the race between them as none of the local jockeys were remotely competent. Dick noticed a small wizened man listening to the conversation. Between the last two fences Freeman looked the winner, but the old man Dick had noticed ranged up on his mount and, leaning over, calmly removed the bridle from Freeman's horse.

'Now let's see you ride a finish, sonny,' he remarked with a chuckle as he drove his mount to the finishing post, leaving the two southern jockeys absolutely flabbergasted!

Pacemaker, **1979**.

Michael Dickinson

You may have noticed that I very rarely hit horses. I love horses and I hate hitting them. I reckon that if you hit a horse twice then next time you will have to hit him three times and so on. It's a vicious circle.

MICHAEL DICKINSON, **1974**.

I think that trainers who are always changing jockeys are not so lucky, nor are their horses.

MICHAEL DICKINSON.

I can't talk about anything other than horses. I don't go out much and I'm only happy doing everything to help me win more races. It is a way of life.

MICHAEL DICKINSON.

Frenchie Nicholson told me I'd never make a jockey. He said with my size I should make a good window cleaner and my legs would save me the trouble of buying a ladder.

MICHAEL DICKINSON, **1975**.

I will not tolerate misuse of the whip by our lads. I won twenty-three races on Dorlesa, and never had to hit her once.

MICHAEL DICKINSON, **1981**.

The difference between being brilliant and ending up on the ground is a very thin line.

MICHAEL DICKINSON, **1983**.

Steve Donoghue

'How did he go?'
'If you'd been on your honeymoon, you couldn't have had a happier time.'

STEVE DONOGHUE after winning one of his six Queen Alexandras on Brown Jack.

Jack Dowdeswell

Jack Dowdeswell was downing a gin and tonic or two in the local after the hospital had discharged him, when Dave Dick swaggered (there is no other word for the way Dave walks) into the pub.
'How did you get on, Jack?' he asked. For once Jack was embarrassed. He blushed deep red and stammered in that deep bass: 'I had to have fifteen stitches in, my old man.'
'Fifteen stitches?' shouted Dave in a voice that echoed round the bar. 'You're boasting!'

TIM FITZGEORGE-PARKER in *Steeplechase Jockeys, The Great Ones*.

Pat Eddery

But if it's no good I tell them [owners] straight. There are a lot of jockeys who don't. But I would be the last to blame them because they're freelance and they are only saying good things because they want to ride it again.

PAT EDDERY, **1974**.

It may have been tough, but it was worth every drop of sweat.

PAT EDDERY on his apprenticeship with Frenchie Nicholson, **1984**.

I've never read the form book and don't need it.

PAT EDDERY, the *Sun*.

What I'm getting is between me and my bank manager.

PAT EDDERY, **1980**.

Brian Fletcher

I reckon 97 out of every 100 jump jockeys would earn more in a factory.

BRIAN FLETCHER, **1977**.

George Fordham

When I get down to the post on those two-year-olds, and I feel their little hearts beating under my legs I think, why not let them have an easy race, win if they can but don't frighten them.

GEORGE FORDHAM.

Jim Fox

It does not worry me that I'll never be a top jockey, another Terry Biddlecombe or Richard Pitman, I enjoy riding and I've no regrets. In almost any job you will get to the top if you are good enough, but not in racing. You can be a good and skilful jockey and get nowhere.

JIM FOX, *News of the World*.

Dick Francis

I am firmly against women riding in National Hunt races. . . . I would deny them the equal right to cripple their limbs or disfigure their faces. Jump racing is as physically wrong for girls as is boxing.

DICK FRANCIS, **1972**.

John Francome

I like the game but I am not obsessed by it. If something came along which could earn us more money, I would stop tomorrow.

JOHN FRANCOME, *Sunday Times*, **1975**.

Being a champion over the sticks isn't a patch on the same thing on the Flat. It's a different class, not even second class - more like working class.

JOHN FRANCOME, **1977**.

Memories are fine but if, at the end of the road, that's all you've got – they can become a bit threadbare.

JOHN FRANCOME.

Most jockeys I know would have sex on the morning of the Grand National if they could.

JOHN FRANCOME.

I don't think I'm brilliant at anything. I'd just sum myself up by saying that I'm very competent.

JOHN FRANCOME, **1982**

John Francome was sometimes too outspoken for his own good. His bluntness could make your eyes water.

MONTY COURT, The *Weekender*, **1985**.

I doubt if there has ever been a rider with more finesse than him.

PETER SCUDAMORE on John Francome, **1987**.

Josh Gifford

'God, I need a fall,' he said earnestly. 'I'm really due one. I haven't come off since Hello Dolly the day after Boxing Day. I must have gone more than sixty rides without one. I want one badly.'

JOSH GIFFORD, talking to Hugh McIlvanney in the *Observer*, **1967**.

Adam Gordon

> She raced at the rasper, I felt my knees grasp her
> I found my hands give to the strain on the bit
> She rose when the Clown did – our silks as we bounded
> Brush'd lightly, our stirrups clash'd hard as we lit . . .

ADAM LINDSAY GORDON on his victory in the **1847** Cheltenham Grand Annual Steeplechase.

Tommy Gosling

When Tommy Gosling was riding he made the mistake of starting to play a lot of football and so on to strengthen his legs. He finished up with legs like Carnera and once the muscle was there it wouldn't be shifted.

JIMMY LINDLEY on jockeys' weight problems, **1977**.

Eddie Harty

I don't see why jockeys can't bet in races in which they're not involved.

EDDIE HARTY.

Freddie Head

She must be bloody good to win the way Freddie Head rode her.

A press room cynic on Miesque's win in the **1987** 1000 Guineas, quoted by
CHRISTOPHER POOLE.

Edward Hide

Winning a race is ninety-five per cent being on the best horse in
the race.

EDDIE HIDE, **1975**.

When his last season comes, I shan't put him up – he's so sharp
he'd start training for all my owners!

MICK EASTERBY on Edward Hide, **1977**.

Edward Hide was the brainiest jockey to have ridden for me.
Trouble with Eddie was that he jocked himself off so many times
you didn't know until they were down at the start that he was on
yours.

MICK EASTERBY, **1987**.

John Hislop

It has not been unknown for jockeys to ride good races when
drunk but such cases have been in respect of good jockeys who
have succumbed either to dissipation or the necessity of a panacea
for lost nerve; in the former case it seems reasonable to expect
that they would probably have ridden a rather better race sober,
in the latter it is a sign that the end of their career is to hand.
Without claiming to be any authority on the subject I think that
the effect of alcohol on a jockey is to make him think that he is
riding better than he is, and that when he feels the need to avail
himself of 'Dutch Courage' he should retire, before an overgen-
erous dose brings about an interview with the stewards and the
loss of his licence or permit.

JOHN HISLOP in *Steeplechasing*.

Kevin Hodgson

I wasn't bright but I wasn't daft either.

KEVIN HODGSON, **1986**.

Rae Johnstone

He had been a compulsive gambler and, in the thirties, when he was very hard up and living in a tiny bedsitter, he went to ask Wertheimer for his retainer a year in advance. He arrived back an hour later looking very downcast and his wife Mary asked, 'What's wrong? Didn't you get it?' 'Yes,' he said, 'but I've lost it.' He had called in at the casino on the way back and done the lot.

PETER O'SULLEVAN on Rae Johnstone, **1980**.

Rae was a totally honest man. That may sound an absurd thing to say about someone who had pulled horses, but it really wasn't such a grievous crime in those days and it was always done in connivance with the connections and never against those he was riding for.

PETER O'SULLEVAN on Rae Johnstone.

Shaun Keightley

I love the weighing room. It's like a second home to me.

SHAUN KEIGHTLEY.

Paul Kelleway

I'm not a fanny merchant. I don't give owners or trainers the tale. If a horse is a bastard I say so. I may not get the ride but we know where we stand.

PAUL KELLEWAY, the *Observer*, **1969**.

There are a few jockeys who are not very clever, but because they are diplomatic they get some of the best chances. The whole emphasis in this sport is on being able to talk well.

PAUL KELLEWAY.

Jeff King

I have never rung up for a ride in my life. If they want me, they will get me. . . . Too much is made of all this riding over the last and on the run-in. Races are won and lost out in the country. How many photo finishes are there over the jumps? It's more important to be a good horseman than to be especially strong on the run-in. But, of course, it's a help if you can do both.

JEFF KING, the *Sun*.

Women riding at Aintree don't worry me. There will be just as many amateurs going round who will be just as much a pain in the neck.

JEFF KING, the *Sun*.

Geoff Lewis

Most of the time race-riding isn't as desperately arduous, for those who are used to it, as outsiders may imagine.

GEOFF LEWIS, **1977**.

Jimmy Lindley

One day I think you'll see a champion Chinese jockey.

JIMMY LINDLEY, BBC, **1971**.

If you've had breakfast you wish you hadn't. If you haven't you wish you had.

JIMMY LINDLEY.

Jack Lynch

When I rode my first winner for Mr Persse I had weighed out a pound overweight. As I jumped down in the winner's enclosure expecting at least to be told 'well done', what I got was a kick up the backside. 'That's to teach you not to eat too much,' was all the Guv'nor said – and I never did again.

JACK LYNCH.

Elain Mellor

I may sound tough, but I say to woman riders who complain, 'If you don't like the heat, stay out of the kitchen.'

ELAIN MELLOR, lady jockey, **1980**.

That's the difficulty with girl jockeys. It's *not* physical. You find plenty of girls tough enough to ride well against men. But it's girls not being so strong mentally.

ELAIN MELLOR.

Stan Mellor

I was young and fearless in those days, but always enjoyed riding at Cartmel. They used to call me 'Cartmellor', probably because I kept coming back on a stretcher.

STAN MELLOR, **1982**.

I was just a punchy, driving sort of jockey really.

STAN MELLOR, **1984**.

Joe Mercer

They call me Smokey Joe because I've always got a pipe in my mouth.

JOE MERCER, **1979**.

Another reason for the short irons is that in the old days they used to have long lead cloths which came down well below the saddle and brushed your ankles and made them bleed. I got lead poisoning in Jamaica once.

JOE MERCER.

Lord Mildmay

Modest, gay, quizzically resolute, he was the exemplar of a brave and honourable tradition. There never was a harder rider, a better loser or a more popular winner; and although he always valued the race more than the victory and the victory more than the prize, he would not perhaps have disdained the reward he has won – which is a kind of immortality among the English.

The Times obituary to Lord Mildmay, **1950**.

Tim Molony

I've never believed in getting off too soon. I always reckoned to drive my horse on right into the ground – to the point of no return – before ever letting myself fall. You don't have so far to fall.

TIM MOLONY, **1979**.

Gary Moore

You've either got it or you haven't. Your father can't breed it into you.

GARY MOORE, son of the great George, **1986**.

It's common knowledge that jockeys bet in Hong Kong and elsewhere. It still goes on and will always be the same.

GARY MOORE giving evidence in the Hong Kong race-fixing trial.

Tony Murray

If you lose a race it's a matter of passing the buck: the owner blames the trainer, the trainer blames the jockey, the jockey blames the poor old horse.

TONY MURRAY, the *Guardian*.

John Oaksey

In racing there are fools, bloody fools, and men who remount in a steeplechase.

JOHN OAKSEY, in *The Wit of the Turf*.

Just suppose, for instance, that Lester Piggott had been convicted of 'excessive use' after winning the Derby on Roberto or The Minstrel. In both cases his effort added literally millions of pounds to the value of those horses so how on earth could you devise a penalty likely to deter him?

JOHN OAKSEY.

He says he wants to be an amateur, but he's left it a bit late if you ask me.

BOB TURNELL on the twenty-six-year-old John Lawrence, later Lord Oaksey.

Jonjo O'Neill

If I'm going to be champion jockey, it will happen without me worrying about it.

JONJO O'NEILL, **1978**.

When you've ridden a bad race the last thing you want is a bollocking.

JONJO O'NEILL on his apprenticeship with Gordon Richards, **1978**.

That man's a saint.

An Irish racegoer on JONJO O'NEILL, **1978**.

No sex before a race? That's a load of marbles. It doesn't apply to me or any other rider I know.

JONJO O'NEILL.

Keith Piggott

A farmer had asked me to come and ride his horse but somebody had told him that I was going to pull the horse up. So he soaped the reins. They were so slippery that it was all I could do to hold him. I couldn't pull him or anything. I trotted up after making all the running.

KEITH PIGGOTT (Lester's father), **1982**.

Lester Piggott

He relishes each crisp fiver like some jewel, for money is his staff of life and he ekes it out as sparingly as a man faced with fifty years of unpensionable retirement.

BILL RICKABY on Lester Piggott.

In a perfect world, I would have Lester ride for me in all the big races, but in none of the trials.

VINCENT O'BRIEN, *Sunday Times*, **1977**.

Knowing just how far the rules of racing can be bent was part of Lester's job, a part, I guess, which gave him special pleasure.

JOHN OAKSEY, *Daily Telegraph*.

When you are away from home with him and at a hotel and you go in early in the morning, you find him with the *Financial Times* up in front of his face, and a pot of black coffee beside the bed and one of those big cigars in his mouth. He can tell you the exchange rate in any part of the world.

HARRY CARR on Lester Piggott, the *Observer*.

The truth is that Piggott, for all his strength, determination and natural talent, is technically limited, and his inability to use his whip in his left hand and his lack of control over the lateral movements of his mounts through his legs allow them to deviate more often than they should.

PETER WILLETT, *Sporting Chronicle*, **1969**.

The only danger to Nijinsky is the jockey.

LESTER PIGGOTT, **1970**, before the Irish Derby. Piggott was referring to Liam Ward, who two years earlier had been beaten on Sir Ivor in the same race.

People think I'm a millionaire but that's impossible. At the end of the day, I won't get a quarter of the way.

LESTER PIGGOTT, ITV, **1970**.

People ask me why I ride with my bottom in the air. Well, I've got to put it somewhere.

LESTER PIGGOTT, *Coventry Evening Telegraph*.

Lester Piggott would admit, if pressed, that money is not every-thing, but he organizes his life on the basis that it is useful stuff to carry when you go for the groceries.

HUGH MCILVANNEY in *The Wit of the Turf*.

Does Lester have a favourite race? The reply is surprising. He doesn't mention one of the big classical races. 'If I am to be quite honest, I prefer a walk-over.'

KURT ZECHMEISTER, *Turf-Journal*.

What a tremendous jockey. I've never had much of a conversation with him, because he's quiet and never says much. Lester rarely says anything unless it's asking you about a horse. He never asks me about horses I ride now because he knows I won't tell him. But there are jockeys who love talking. The only way they can get near to him is by telling him about such and such a horse and what it's like to ride. He rides it next time. They're mad to tell him. I won't tell him anything. No way. Because for sure he'd pinch it next time.

PAT EDDERY on Lester Piggott, **1974**.

Everyone saw Lester Piggott get Roberto home in the Derby and said it was the mark of a genius. But when another jockey does it, it's a different kettle of fish.

KEN PAYNE, trainer, after his jockey was fined for excessive use of the whip, **1974**.

At what point do you think you definitely had the race won? The winning post.

JULIAN WILSON interviewing Lester Piggott, BBC.

Jeremy Tree quizzed Piggott hard one day. 'I've got to speak to my old school, Lester, all the boys at Eton, and tell them all I know about racing. What shall I say?' . . . again the pause and the muffled reply: 'Tell 'em you have flu.'

TONY LEWIS, *Sunday Telegraph*.

'Parnell, I am asking you to ride for me at Ascot. If you will not, I shall have to engage Lester Piggott.' 'Quite right, my Lord,' came back the answer. 'That has always been my philosophy – if you cannot get the best, get the next best.'

Pacemaker, **1978**.

Lester is a great man at making a horse look twenty lengths better than it is. He'll come there, sit still and only win by a length. Everybody thinks he's got a ton in hand. Lester quite frequently hasn't got anything at all.

JOHN REID on Lester Piggott, **1978**.

He gives the impression that, if he rode facing backwards, he would still win the races that count.

JOHN HISLOP on Lester Piggott in *From Start to Finish*, **1980**.

Not only am I not so deaf now, but I have learnt to lip read and

I watch people's faces. They are more expressive than horses' faces but not so reliable.

LESTER PIGGOTT, **1982**.

One of the great sights in racing is to see Lester go before the stewards. He goes in there like Clint Eastwood – and comes out like Clint Eastwood. He doesn't give a damn.

BRYN CROSSLEY, *Sunday Telegraph* magazine.

He is a genius but I don't want to have to dance to his music.

DANIEL WILDENSTEIN on Lester Piggott, **1984**.

The most famous recipe in racing is the one for Lester Piggott's breakfast – a cough and a copy of *The Sporting Life*.

SIMON BARNES, *The Times*.

St Paddy needed a Lester Piggott to ride him because he ran in panicky snatches and Lester could control the panic.

CLIVE BRITTAIN, **1986**.

Copy Joe Mercer not me, for if you try to ride like me you will end up breaking your neck.

LESTER PIGGOTT, the *Guardian*.

Friday's sentence was no doubt correct because we live in a tamed, interdependent world where non-acceptance can lead to anarchy. Lester was a wild animal, answerable to no-one. Now we've locked him up. That's sad for while it's proven how much he took, no-one will ever assess how much he gave.

BROUGH SCOTT on Lester Piggott's sentence of three years in prison for tax fraud, *Sunday Times*, **1987**.

Lester would be better teaching handicapped children about horses than languishing in an overfilled prison.

GERRY BERMINGHAM MP.

I always think prisons should be for people who are violent or dangerous and have got to be sorted out and prison will do them good. I don't think the actual act of putting Lester in prison will do any good at all; to have taken more money off him would have been more of a punishment and more effective.

He's quite complicated, Lester, and I am not sure he will be able to cope with it. It won't sort him out, but it might break his heart.

SUE MONTGOMERY, profile in *Sporting Life*, **1988**.

I remember Vincent O'Brien saying once that the real charm of having Lester ride for you was that it got him off the other fellow's horse.

CHARLES ST GEORGE, **1988**.

Richard Pitman

I'd never known tiredness like it. People think you're just sitting there, you're not. You're trying to hold the horse together and Crisp was a big, strong bugger.

RICHARD PITMAN on riding Crisp in the 1973 Grand National.

Sir Gordon Richards

In my sixty-three years in racing I have never seen anyone do anything reckless really deliberately.

SIR GORDON RICHARDS, *Sunday Mirror*.

As a matter of fact, I find donkeys very difficult to ride.

SIR GORDON RICHARDS, **1987**.

Every time I held him up Tudor Minstrel fought me. Every time I let him down to go, he shot off to the right. Either way he was making certain that he lost the race. The whole race was a nightmare, but he still finished fourth. I was told that I had pulled the horse's head off. One late night caller had the nerve to tell me that he had found a horse's head and bridle on Tattenham Hill.

SIR GORDON RICHARDS.

Yves St Martin

It is a very good life with horses. I only would like all human people to be like horses. No horses are wrong in racing, only a few of the people in racing are not good.

YVES ST MARTIN.

Michael Scudamore

You've got to do yourself justice and you don't do that by being 'one of the boys' but through single-mindedness and self discipline.

MICHAEL SCUDAMORE.

Peter Scudamore

Of course, like everybody I drop it occasionally, but I can do everything with a stick.

PETER SCUDAMORE, **1981**.

I would probably never make a Flat jockey, as much as I would love to.

PETER SCUDAMORE.

I don't think that I have ever modelled myself on anybody. I just ride.

PETER SCUDAMORE.

The day when you come in and you don't know why you've fallen, that is when you start worrying.

PETER SCUDAMORE.

Perhaps some people would not agree that I am the world's greatest stylist after the last, but nobody has ever told me that I am weak in a finish.

PETER SCUDAMORE.

As father says, when you get a horse on the floor, nine times out of ten it's the rider's fault because you are faced with a decision, and, when you finish on the floor, it is obvious that you have made the wrong decision.

PETER SCUDAMORE.

I don't care if you are Lester Piggott, if you have got your horse running, the only thing you can do is to keep him running.

PETER SCUDAMORE.

Stupidly I love the game. I would do it for less.

PETER SCUDAMORE, **1986**.

Peter deserves to succeed because he works so hard at it, but he is also better at his job through learning there is more to life than racing.

MICHAEL SCUDAMORE on his son, Peter, *Mail on Sunday*, **1986**.

You need determination, concentration and the will to win, and I believe you can communicate these things to horses.

PETER SCUDAMORE, **1987**.

People say I look miserable. I don't feel miserable. It's just concentration.

PETER SCUDAMORE.

Neville Sellwood

Neville Sellwood was perhaps the greatest jockey ever. Riders often lose races they should have won, but he won ones he shouldn't.

ALEC HEAD, **1975**.

I tried to talk to him but it was no good. He died in my arms. A part of me died that day too. It was a tragedy that broke me up inside. I changed my racing colours from that day so no other rider would ever have to wear the silks he died in.

ALEC HEAD on the death of his jockey, Neville Sellwood, **1975**.

Willie Shoemaker

This jockey told me that he came wide on the bend because if he came between horses the stewards would have taken the race off him. I told him that Shoemaker would have won on the horse. He asked me why. I told him that Shoemaker would have won the race how he could and have worried about the stewards later. I told him that that was why Shoemaker is a champion and he's not.

JOHN NERUD, American trainer.

I think more horses are whipped out of the money than into it.

WILLIE SHOEMAKER, **1978**.

I figured the more I listened and less I talked, the better off I'd be.

WILLIE SHOEMAKER.

Tommy Shone

I can see Tommy [Shone] now sitting on the scales saying to old Manning, the clerk of the scales, 'I wasn't third. I wasn't in the first eighteen!' But Manning replied: 'According to my ticket you were third.' He was weighed in and it still stands in the book.

BOB TURNELL, **1982**.

Charlie Smirke

Very few jockeys have been really generous, but Charlie Smirke was one of them. He was a character but a very particular man.

If he saw a little piece of cotton on his breeches he'd pick it off straight away.

FRED DYER, jockey's valet, **1984**.

The test of a good jockey isn't the races he should win; it's the ones he wins that he shouldn't win.

CHARLIE SMIRKE.

Bill Smith

On the Flat, you see idiot jockeys knocking the daylights out of their horses. They are really whip happy and it makes me wince. I will do anything to avoid whipping a horse.

BILL SMITH, the *Sun*.

Steve Smith-Eccles

I like a lazy horse, one who wants a bit of chasing.

STEVE SMITH-ECCLES, **1979**.

The game is no good if they can't jump, and I think it is tremendously satisfying to be in on starting a young horse to jump, teaching him your way and then carrying it off in a race.

STEVE SMITH-ECCLES.

I had this ability to learn things very quick but then I used to start messing about.

STEVE SMITH-ECCLES.

There are two versions of how the double barrel got into the name. Steve prefers a romantic tale straight out of *The Importance of Being Earnest* about his grandfather being found in a bag on the vicar's doorstep.

BROUGH SCOTT on Steve Smith-Eccles.

In this job, you need a good woman to look after you. If she didn't cook and wash and clean, I would never get any of it done. By the end of a day's riding and driving, I'm in no state for any of that.

STEVE SMITH-ECCLES.

I got the shoulders humping sacks of coal around in my school-days, helping a mate who had a private coal delivery business.

STEVE SMITH-ECCLES, the *Guardian*, **1986**.

Tommy Stack

When the butler met me off the plane, I knew nobody in racing.

TOMMY STACK on his arrival in England to ride for Bobby Renton.

Greville Starkey

I'm in it for the money. The more money I make, the better I can live. I'd like to make ten times more money than I have already. Then I could retire and play golf.

GREVILLE STARKEY, **1978**.

If Greville Starkey ever puts his neck out turning round on any of my horses you can say that I'd be very happy to pay for any treatment he'd need to get it straight.

TERRY RAMSDEN, **1986**.

It becomes increasingly difficult to persuade Americans of the respect in which Greville Starkey is held in Britain. There is a growing belief in the USA that he is always left three lengths in the stalls. On Roussillon he did nothing to alter this impression.

PAUL HAIGH on the **1985** Breeders' Cup.

He is an enormously good judge of distance.

GUY HARWOOD on his stable jockey, Greville Starkey, **1983**.

Brian Taylor

When you're thirty-five and things are not going well, you know that the bad times will change into the good. When you're forty-five, you're not so sure.

BRIAN TAYLOR, **1984**.

Ryan Price sent his assistant to go and get his betting slip. I won't say how much he had on but it was a lot at 25 to 1. Harry Demetriou looked at the ticket and saw that the bet was each way. 'But I thought you said he'd win,' he said. That didn't shake the Captain at all. 'That's just in case the jockey makes a balls-up,' he said, looking straight at me.

BRIAN TAYLOR.

Arthur Thompson

I have never yet let a horse on the run-in slip through on my inside, nor will I ever do.

ARTHUR THOMPSON, quoted by Jim Snow.

Brent Thompson

Because of the tight way of racing in Australia, with the horses very close together, if you don't get suspended now and then, you're either lucky or not showing much drive.

BRENT THOMPSON, **1984**.

John Thorne

I always wanted to swim the Channel and ride in the National, but I was too fat for the National and too thin for the Channel.

JOHN THORNE, who did later ride Spartan Missile into second place in the 1981 Grand National.

Colin Tinkler

When [Colin] Tinkler said that the part of the Catterick race not visible on television showed Carnival Day to be an inadequate jumper of fences, it was no surprise that questioning stopped abruptly once it was established he was riding at Nottingham that day.

HOWARD WRIGHT on Michael Dickinson's successful libel action against the *Racing Specialist*.

Andy Turnell

Riding very short is much better when your horse falls. Nine times out of ten you are catapulted clear. If you're riding longer and start sitting too tight, sort of glued to the saddle, you can get well and truly buried.

ANDY TURNELL.

Bob Turnell

Both hands on the reins. You can't ride with two let alone one.

BOB TURNELL, trainer, to his jockey son, Andy, **1987**.

Once between the mane and tail you're a fixture, not a picture.

BOB TURNELL.

He was a terrific horseman and up until his death he would ride anything, no matter how difficult. If something wanted a ride, he'd be the man to do it.

ANDY TURNELL, trainer, on his father Bob Turnell, **1987**.

He rode his first winner when he was sixteen, and his second when he was twenty-seven.

ANDY TURNELL on his father.

Jorge Velasquez

American people don't like the English style – real high in the
saddle and the feet all the way in the stirrups.

JORGE VELASQUEZ, top American jockey, **1981**.

Lorna Vincent

I'm not in any rush to get married yet, although I would not like
to leave it much later than twenty-five. Racing is not as romantic
as many people think.

LORNA VINCENT, *Evening Mail*, **1979**.

Fred Winter

'I shouldn't bother to tell Winter anything,' Sir Winston interrupts
in his booming voice [to Christopher Soames giving instructions
at Sandown]. 'You are talking to a master of his craft.'

JANE MCILVANE, American author, in *The Will to Win*.

Harry Wragg

You can't count on your best friend. You think 'Oh, I'm all right
– old so-and-so would never do me' – and then old so-and-so not
only cuts you off like a thistle, but can't even remember doing it
afterwards.

HARRY WRAGG, *Horse and Hound*.

I nearly always thought I could run before I could walk.

HARRY WRAGG on his early years as an apprentice.

That bugger should be head waiter at the Café Royal.

Anonymous punter on HARRY WRAGG, giving him his eternal nickname.

If a racehorse could talk, one of the first things he'd tell his jockey would be 'If you don't know where the bloody winning post is, I'm sure I don't.'

HARRY WRAGG, **1978**.

All jockeys make mistakes, good jockeys make fewest.

HARRY WRAGG.

5
Trainers

My trainers say I'm impossible but they come on bicycles and leave in Bentleys.

MAJOR LIONEL HOLLIDAY in *The Epsom Derby*.

The standard of permit holders ranges from the select handful who have forgotten more than many professional trainers will ever know, through a large and perfectly competent majority down to those in whose operations neither the rules of racing, the science of training nor for that matter the Ten Commandments play any significant part.

JOHN OAKSEY, *Sunday Telegraph*, **1969**.

It is this art of the professional trainer which is going to be progressively sought now by owners faced with the daunting prospect of paying £45 per week by the end of the season.

Pacemaker editorial, **1974**, not anticipating the £200 per week being charged by some trainers in 1988.

The men and women who have their horses trained at Newmarket are the meanest. Owners who patronise Epsom stables are the sexiest.

CLIVE GRAHAM.

If you know horses, you understand the trainer's problems. If I have a bad horse, I want to know. You can't make a good horse out of a bad one. All the trainers I've been with have been good, but some are better than others.

CAPTAIN MARCOS LEMOS, **1975**.

Bank manager required by frustrated trainer wishing to expand. Should be genuine, game, consistent and capable of carrying weight.

Advertisement in *The Sporting Life*, **1978**.

The best day for a trainer to win a race is Friday.

IVOR HERBERT on the best opportunity for press coverage.

There was one amusing side for those old enough to remember the fight to bring stalls to our racecourses. It was the trainers who put up the strongest opposition, yet this week it was the trainers who were loudest in their condemnation of their absence.

RICHARD BAERLEIN, **1979**.

It's the small trainers who keep you going. Stick with the little people. They want to win races and so do I. They have to work three times as hard as top trainers with money behind them.

BRIAN ROUSE, **1979**.

Trainers by nature are seldom savers. Eat, drink and be merry. . . . Tomorrow we're bankrupt.

IVOR HERBERT, **1980**.

Contrary to their public image of popping corks for landed owners, jumping trainers do not make money.

IVOR HERBERT, ex-jumping trainer, **1980**.

The story goes that the trainer wished the child to receive the name of Ballyboggan (second in the 1919 Grand National) but his wife not surprisingly drew the line at that. In the end a compromise was reached and the boy was given the name of Aintree.

ROGER MORTIMER, **1983**.

When you're a struggling jockey, you can get by. If you're a struggling trainer, you sink.

BRUCE RAYMOND, *The Sporting Life*.

Robert Armstrong

I do like horses with brains. The worst thing anyone can do is to send me a horse that is stupid.

ROBERT ARMSTRONG.

Ian Balding

If there were no whips at all I would not mind.

IAN BALDING.

George Beeby

Lambourn in the afternoon always reminds me of a mining village on strike.

GEORGE BEEBY, **1977**.

Sir Cecil Boyd-Rochfort

You seem to have no faith in me, like all your other trainers, and I certainly do not intend to be treated in this way. . . . You may think you may be a great judge of your own business, but you certainly know nothing about horses. You have the finest stable in America, but you are making nothing except a mess of it, and I should be ashamed to have had so many trainers in the last few years.

SIR CECIL BOYD-ROCHFORT, writing to Mrs Elizabeth Arden Graham.

Clive Brittain

When people have done well, others tend to forget they started with nothing. We all start with nothing – some people have talent and some have money behind them, but at the end of the day in this game, unless you work and unless you are dedicated, you just don't last.

CLIVE BRITTAIN, *The European Racehorse*, **1983**.

I wouldn't make much of a writer but I don't do too badly as a trainer.

CLIVE BRITTAIN.

I regard him as a very good trainer, largely underestimated, and absolutely straight – he's never even thought of doing anything he shouldn't.

MAJOR DAVID SWANNELL, former Jockey Club handicapper on Clive Brittain, **1986**.

Tim Brookshaw

Already the man who was paralysed from the waist down is schooling his horses. 'The guv'nor's a marvel,' said his stable lad Arthur Bevan. 'Every time he jumps a hurdle or fence I hold my breath. Another fall on the spine could kill him. But he just laughs and says he is still happiest of all when he is riding.'

JACK WOOD on Tim Brookshaw, the *Sun*.

Dai Burchell

It's true what Murless used to say about people slapping their horses when they returned to the winner's enclosure – all they need is a nice little tap, you don't want to hear it echoing back up the road.

DAI BURCHELL, The *Weekender*.

Henry Candy

I never like getting involved with racing politics. I leave other people to talk about that sort of thing and take the dogs for a walk.

HENRY CANDY.

Jack Cann

There's a lot of chaps trainin' today that never learned the art of feedin'. Some o' ours get four feeds a day. And they've a little mash fed to 'em coming back in the box from the races.

JACK CANN, *Sunday Express*, **1975**.

Henry Cecil

There's a world of difference between training at Newmarket and in Berkshire. You work the horses much faster and quicken up more at the finish. Cecil likes to find out the time of day. If they're not good enough to finish in the first three first time out, they just don't run.

JOE MERCER, *The Field*.

Nauseating – that is how I describe the huge sums of money being flung into the market for yearlings. If this stupid spending could be curbed in the next ten years, racing would do itself a real service. It is so unrealistic. And often the people responsible are not the backbone of the sport.

HENRY CECIL, **1979**.

Trainers who spend time prostituting themselves at cocktail parties get the owners they deserve.

HENRY CECIL.

To be happy a horse must be relaxed. If not, he's no good. You can beat a 'bad' horse – hit him when he rears or stops at home. But you can't *cure* him that way. And on the racecourse he'll always have the last laugh on you.

HENRY CECIL, **1982**.

You can correct – usually – horses that have been abused. We enjoy that challenge. You have to be a sort of psychiatrist. You must get that horse to think: 'People here are nice to us, so we'll start being nice to them.'

HENRY CECIL.

I don't suppose God cares very much if you get done in a race at Wolverhampton.

HENRY CECIL.

I wouldn't even go down the road to race if we didn't have a horse running.

HENRY CECIL.

The nicest thing about training is going out with the horses in the morning and going round them in the evening.

HENRY CECIL.

Cecil's strike rate owes much to the fact that he will not run animals that fail to show ability at home.

PETER JONES on Henry Cecil, **1982**.

Stamina is either there or it isn't. You don't make it. You can't.

HENRY CECIL, **1982**.

When things are going well everyone wants to know you. But in two years' time they walk by as if you were a lamppost.

HENRY CECIL, *Sunday Telegraph*, **1983**.

You couldn't call me eccentric. Childish, maybe, a backward mentality.

HENRY CECIL, *The Times*.

Of course you've got to have a certain amount of ambition and ruthlessness or you become an also-ran. If you haven't got the burning wish to beat everyone in sight, you've had it. I'm a jealous man by nature. Some people I'm pleased to see doing well, but others I'm definitely not.

HENRY CECIL.

A lot of people think you can train a horse on the racecourse. 'Run him, he needs the race, doesn't matter, he'll win next time.' I don't think that works. The horse, if he's genuine, he's doing his best, he gets tired and he's got two furlongs to go and his lungs are hurting him and he's beginning to hate it, although he wants to do it. I don't see how the next time he can be in the right frame of mind.

HENRY CECIL, *Racing World*, **1988**.

If you let a horse down too much sometimes he just doesn't come back.

HENRY CECIL.

It used to amuse me to wear outrageous clothes, but I've grown out of that a bit now. But I like to make a joke of myself.

If you do that then you've got people off guard and it's easier. They think you're a fool and then you move in. If they're wary of you then you've got no chance, have you?

SUE MONTGOMERY, profile in *The Sporting Life*.

Paul Cole

If I see a boy has the right attitude and rides well. I can give him opportunities in public. Then he needs luck and plenty of it.

PAUL COLE, **1982**.

Jack Colling

Give me a stable full of geldings and I will have the bookmakers crying for mercy.

JACK COLLING, **1970**.

Con Collins

All this evening racing makes it difficult to get as much fishing as I should like.

CON COLLINS, **1978**.

Neville Crump

I remember we were staying at the Midland in Manchester and we pushed Jack Hilton into the laundry basket. Took him to the cleaners, you could say.

NEVILLE CRUMP, **1985**.

Shining Gold was a great leaper, and I remember how he proved it one day at Carlisle, when Arthur Thompson really put him to the test. Guy Cunard's horse had refused and Guy was lying there in a heap on top of the fence. 'Keep still and you'll be alright,' shouted Arthur, and he was. Shining Gold sailed over them both quite easily.

NEVILLE CRUMP.

That evening my host, the senior Steward of the meeting, asked me how long I'd been schooling my horses in public and I told him, 'Oh, for about forty-seven years!'

NEVILLE CRUMP.

Fred Darling

'Where's Mr Darling?' Miss Dorothy Paget asked Gordon Richards after he dismounted from Colonel Payne after the Cork and Orrery.
   'I wouldn't be sure,' Gordon replied, 'but I've a shrewd idea he's on the top of the stand cutting his throat.'

DOROTHY PAGET on Fred Darling, in *Queen of the Turf – The Dorothy Paget Story*.

He was a little Tartar for detail, and, during the two years I was with him, there was not one single day when I failed to get a rousting for something. It was usually for the most minute flaw in my work and, at the time, it nearly drove me mad.
   But it did give me the perception to note at a quick glance if a martingale was too tight or too loose, if a bit was too high in the mouth or any of the hundred and one things that a trainer needs to spot instantly.

MARCUS MARSH on Fred Darling.

Michael Dickinson

I want to do one job and do it well. The better prize money on the Flat is no lure, I would sooner be happy and successful in what I am doing now than be a miserable millionaire.

MICHAEL DICKINSON, the *Sun*.

I definitely think he should stick to National Hunt. As I keep telling him I don't think he'd like Flat racers.

MICHAEL STOUTE on Michael Dickinson, *Daily Telegraph*, **1983**.

Horses definitely benefit from easy races; there is no point in subjecting them to a severe test until it really matters.

MICHAEL DICKINSON, **1983**.

To get the best out of your children, particularly if you work together, has long been one of the supreme tests of parenthood. That's why there was a challenge as well as a chuckle when Tony Dickinson looked across at Michael and said: 'Do you think that Sangster knows what he's getting?'

BROUGH SCOTT, **1984**.

John Dunlop

Actually, I must have trained Shirley Heights extremely badly because it's taken all this time and four races to get him fit.

JOHN DUNLOP, *The Times*, **1978**.

I suppose if anything I could be accused of not working my horses hard enough. I hardly ever send them more than six or seven furlongs.

JOHN DUNLOP, *The Field*.

Mick Easterby

Beaches are death traps. I wouldn't dream of exercising any of my horses on the sand.

MICK EASTERBY.

If you can find me a dentist who'll supply a set of dentures that fit, you can tell him I'll train him a horse for nowt.

MICK EASTERBY.

If I can't take it with me, I don't want to go.

Inscription in MICK EASTERBY's office.

It's brains that wins races. I don't give a bugger about style.

MICK EASTERBY, 1977.

I never knew that I was actually riding a horse for Mick [Easterby] until I saw my name on the runners' board.

EDWARD HIDE, 1987.

Our Peter's the brainy one in the family, that's why I like to mix with him. If you associate with sharp-minded people they'll keep you on your toes, whereas if you socialise with half-wits you'll be brought down to their level.

MICK EASTERBY, 1987.

The worst horse I've trained? It was one called Mick'n'Dick. I had half of him with a neighbouring farmer and Dick got so geed up as his debut approached he didn't sleep for four nights and arrived at the racecourse shaking like a leaf from head to foot. We didn't make the first ten then and we didn't make the first ten ever. The consolation was that after his fourth run Dick was sleeping sound as a bell.

MICK EASTERBY.

Everything's for sale around here, even me.

MICK EASTERBY.

Peter Easterby

He went to his first sale on a push-bike. You couldn't make a much humbler start than that.

PAT MULDOON, owner, on Peter Easterby.

No legs, no horse.

PETER EASTERBY.

Bill Elsey

If necessary owners will have to refuse to run their horses to show the Government how much revenue they would miss without racing.

BILL ELSEY, **1975**.

I was actually circling York racecourse in a Spitfire when our stable was winning the Ebor down below.

BILL ELSEY, **1981**.

I can't go down to Annabel's club and chat up people all night, saying they'd better have a horse with me. I'm not that sort of person.

BILL ELSEY, **1985**.

David Elsworth

That's one reason why I dislike all this unnecessary shouting at lads and horses to which ex-cavalry officers are particularly prone. I'm not saying that there can never be a time to go through the roof. But, as a permanent method of communication, it's self-defeating and unintelligent.

DAVID ELSWORTH.

Tim Forster

One day I'm going to stand for Parliament and if I get in, my first Bill will be about abolishing Flat racing and my second about doing away with hurdlers.

TIM FORSTER.

Keep remounting.

TIM FORSTER's last words of advice to Charlie Fenwick before he won the **1980** Grand National on Ben Nevis.

David Gandolfo

I don't bet often but any trainer who tells you that he doesn't bet is either a fool or a liar.

DAVID GANDOLFO, the *Sun*.

Sam Hall

You never get nowt in racing in a hurry.

SAM HALL, **1977**.

Hubert Hartigan

One day a horse choked badly on a carrot. Hubert never hesitated. He took a penknife from his pocket, there and then cut a hole in its throat, removed the carrot and saved the animal's life. 'Can you imagine any modern trainer doing that?' asked the Guv'nor. 'Hubert was a real man – a hell of a man.'

NOEL MURLESS on Hubert Hartigan, in *The Guv'nor*.

Guy Harwood

If you've got the choice of four or five thousand yearlings, and you work hard at it, you must buy nicer horses than if you're limited to the studs of your owners.

GUY HARWOOD, **1983**.

Alec Head

I try not to glance back at the past but forward to the future.

ALEC HEAD, **1975**.

Barry Hills

Yes, I do love fillies. I don't treat them much differently to the colts, once they're in work, but I am easier on them at the start of the season. I've done well with them, so people send me more.

BARRY HILLS, *Mail on Sunday*.

The trainer was silent; lost in thought as his string jogged by on the windy Berkshire hillside. Each one in turn came under his scrutiny until the impeccably-bred crocodile had wended its way down to the cantering ground.

Then he turned, rubbed his hands together, and with a grin that threatened to split his face in two, said: 'My God, we're going to make some money this year.'

COLIN FLEETWOOD-JONES on Barry Hills, **1974**.

Jeremy Hindley

When I say that the professionals are subsidising the industry and keeping it alive, I don't just mean stable lads. Officials, lads, jockeys, trainers are all working for less than they are worth. I tell you, it won't go on for ever, we'll get fewer and fewer good people.

JEREMY HINDLEY, **1980**.

Bruce Hobbs

If I had my way I'd throw all the hypodermic needles into the Atlantic.

BRUCE HOBBS on drugs.

Reg Hollinshead

All my boys know that I cannot stand pointless use of the whip. All boys are prone to it mainly because they follow the bad example of many senior jockeys. But sometimes it's because an owner has been at them in the paddock telling them 'not to be afraid to give it one'. That sort of thing makes my blood boil.

REG HOLLINSHEAD.

Jack Jarvis

Jack Jarvis admitted one great failure: 'I never made a gentleman of Lester Piggott.'

From *The Epsom Derby*.

Ryan Jarvis

I hope you haven't brought anything other than your toothbrush.

RYAN JARVIS to Dick Hern, after he was appointed trainer to Major L. B. Holliday who had a notorious turnover in his trainers, *Pacemaker*, **1979**.

I remember Major Petch's father was auctioneer at Catterick after one of mine won a seller. I was trying to buy it in and he kept bidding it up. In the end I accused him of taking bids off the top deck of a bus going by on the Great North Road.

RYAN JARVIS, **1979**.

Tom Jones

Idle man's way of keeping horses, isn't it?

TOM JONES on feeding horse cubes.

I've only once had a horse pulled on me. Only once *known* it, though I've suspected it sometimes.

TOM JONES, **1981**.

Paul Kelleway

One thing is sure – there is no money to be made from training fees. And I am not going to work my guts out only for an owner to come along one day and take his horse down the road.

PAUL KELLEWAY, **1978**.

I've a reputation as a terrible man to work for. I say what I think.

PAUL KELLEWAY, **1983**.

George Lambton

I take some pride in your stables, and if it is run at a loss, I feel that it is a disgrace.

GEORGE LAMBTON to 17th Earl of Derby in *Classic Connections*.

D. Wayne Lukas

The value of time; the success of perseverance; the pleasure of working; the dignity of simplicity; the worth of character; the power of kindness; the influence of example; the obligation of duty; the wisdom of economy; the virtue of patience; the improvement of talent; the joy of originating.

A sign in the office of American trainer D. WAYNE LUKAS.

Consciously or unconsciously the good trainers are into a programme where they're preparing those horses mentally to perform at their peaks – and I think that's highly overlooked by a lot of trainers.

D. WAYNE LUKAS, **1987**.

Some people train week to week. Some people train day to day. We train minute to minute.

D. WAYNE LUKAS.

Ginger McCain

If a horse has ability you can train it up the side of a mountain or down a mineshaft.

GINGER MCCAIN, **1978**.

Bryan McMahon

Trainers can be thick. You haven't got to have brains to be a trainer, you've just got to have horses.

BRYAN MCMAHON, The *Weekender*, **1986**.

Peter Makin

It's quite ridiculous to say that you can't make it pay. As long as you don't let the overheads run away you can do it. The trouble is, so many trainers aren't businessmen as well. I also make my betting pay, though I'm not what you'd call a gambling trainer.

PETER MAKIN, **1971**.

Doug Marks

I have been everything in racing except a horse.

DOUG MARKS, **1975**.

In a few years' time, half the horses in training in England will be owned by syndicates.

DOUG MARKS, **1975**.

Syd Mercer

I'm not a qualified vet but, believe me son, I can lick 'em all.

SYD MERCER, **1977**.

I had a very fast mare, Wayside Singer, in the early 50's, who I entered in a race at Pontefract one Saturday. I also had a horse called Young Vigorous in the same race.

The mare was set to give the colt a couple of stone, so I took them both to Warwick racecourse one morning and galloped them together. The mare beat the colt a head in 59 seconds, giving him a stone. I knew I was on a cert!

At that time Ernie Davey had one of the best sprinters in the north – Fair Seller – who had won the Ayr Gold Cup. A few days before the 'Ponte' race he rang me up to ask me if I was going to run Wayside Singer. I told him no, but before I could say I was running something else, he put the phone down probably thinking that the only danger to Fair Seller was out of the way.

When I arrived for the race I sent Young Vigorous into the paddock with a plain 'M' on his sheet. They didn't put trainers' names on the racecard in those days. I used 'SM' on most of my sheets and one of my horses would be instantly recognized by that. People came up to me and asked what I was doing at Pontefract and I replied that I was just having a day out.

The joint owner and myself went into the ring to find he was 25–1. We backed him to win £8,000 in eight seconds.

Young Vigorous flew in and broke the course record in the process.'

SYD MERCER, **1974**.

David Morley

You will never catch me walking under a ladder.

DAVID MORLEY.

None of my owners bet and neither do I. It makes life much easier.

DAVID MORLEY, **1979**.

'Mouse' Morris

God is a bookmaker. All the touches people try. They never come off. Something happens.

'MOUSE' MORRIS, **1983**.

Noel Murless

It is a very small point with me. I run very few horses in blinkers. But the freedom of decision is being taken away from owners all the time and I feel that owners are getting a raw deal out of this new legislation. What we are coming to now is that the whole thing is done for the stay-at-home punter. After all it is the owner who pays.

NOEL MURLESS, referring to legislation on declaring blinkers at the overnight stage, *The Sporting Life*, **1972**.

In my life I have had four 'greats' – Abernant, Petite Etoile, Crepello and Sir Gordon Richards.

NOEL MURLESS, **1975**.

Mrs Florence Nagle

I am not a woman's libber. I believe in equal opportunity. But men have always resented us butting in.

MRS FLORENCE NAGLE, **1979**.

John Nerud

I don't actually keep them fat, but looking well. I like a horse to be in a happy frame of mind and I like to see them cantering with freedom on a long rein, contented. I don't rely too much on the clock because I am more interested in the way a horse does his work, not how fast he does it.

JOHN NERUD, American trainer, **1974**.

When I was just starting to train a big stable, Ben Jones of Calumet Farm, whom I shall always regard as the greatest American trainer of my time, visited me and said, 'Son, you don't have enough sense to train these horses, so here's what you do. Keep them fat, and work them half a mile and they will win in spite of you,' and I have never changed my mode.

JOHN NERUD.

Steve Norton

It's very difficult to know as much about your horse without a retained jockey.

STEVE NORTON, **1981**.

Forty horses is the most that any one man can handle properly –
I don't care who he is – and if you've got eighty you need another
man as good as yourself.

STEVE NORTON.

Vincent O'Brien

A horse is like a car. He has only got a certain mileage. The
difficulty is to discover the amount of that mileage.

VINCENT O'BRIEN.

I once saw him with a horse that had an excellent chance of
winning a certain race but shortly before it Vincent noticed some
long hairs around the horse's jawbone. 'No,' he said, 'the horse
is not coated properly. He is not ready to run yet. I will give him
another few weeks.' When the horse did run, he won in a canter.
And that is just how meticulous he is – he bothers with things so
small that the average trainer would not even notice them.

JOHNNY ROE on Vincent O'Brien, 1975.

Edward O'Grady

I believe that if a horse is fed enough and worked enough, he will
not be bored. Horses do not read newspapers, they don't get in
a state if *The Sporting Life* or the *Financial Times* has not arrived.
They are quite happy doing nothing.

EDWARD O'GRADY.

Sally Oliver

If you don't win by ten lengths don't bother pulling up. Just keep
on going and drown yourself in the Trent.

SALLY OLIVER to jockey Paul Barton, who duly won by the required distance, 1986.

Dick Peacock

What I want to see above all else is a two-year-old with a good mouth. This is the vital thing; it can be the be-all or end-all of a horse's career. And to make a good mouth, you have to have a lad with good hands and unlimited patience.

DICK PEACOCK, *The Times*.

Matt Peacock

Gallop 'em for brass. They gallop for nowt at home and that is no bloody good to anybody.

MATT PEACOCK.

Angel Penna

There just some people make less mistake than others, that's all. I at the top, yes. How I do it? What trainer you know go four different countries and keep winning in them all? I take best from every country I train in and put it all together. That the secret. And I can go back any time and do it again.

ANGEL PENNA, **1975**.

Honey, honey, this is America. You never look forward, never. Race is Saturday, you run Saturday. Race is next week, you run next week.

ANGEL PENNA to Juliette Harrison, **1985**.

I like it more the European style, but maybe I do adapt. Oh definitely you put more speed in them. Definitely, or you are dead.

ANGEL PENNA on training in America, **1985**.

Atty Persse

A jumping trainer is a man who trains horses to jump – not fall.

ATTY PERSSE, quoted by Tim Fitzgeorge-Parker.

Keith Piggott

Keith Piggott remembers one morning on the heath when a bystander was talking to Fred 'Rick' Rickaby. A batch of horses came thundering along. 'I suppose that's what they call a half-speed,' he said. 'Yes,' said Rick, 'but it would take them a long time to find the other half.'

TIM FITZGEORGE-PARKER.

I had some rotten animals to train. They were useless and I could do what I liked with them. So I put them in sellers. Luckily, I had a little one that Lester could turn inside-out called The Chase.

KEITH PIGGOTT on his son's first winner.

We decided to run him down the course all through the season to teach him to jump properly. Just like Uncle Charlie used to do.

KEITH PIGGOTT on his 1963 Grand National winner Ayala.

Martin Pipe

Nowadays the bookies don't give you a chance. And, anyway, I'm far too busy to bet.

MARTIN PIPE, the *Independent*.

Jenny Pitman

It's not a big ego trip for me. Just the satisfaction of showing that if someone gives me the goods I can deliver.

JENNY PITMAN, **1981**.

If you want to get rich, Flat racing is your scene. But if you want to be happy, steeplechasing is the thing.

JENNY PITMAN.

If you want to understand the effect of weight on a horse try running for a bus with nothing in your hands. Then try doing it again with your hands full of shopping. Then think about doing that for four and a half miles.

JENNY PITMAN, **1985**.

If I get hold of the man who wrote the rubbish that Burrough Hill Lad would not race again there is every chance of him being castrated.

JENNY PITMAN, referring to her horse's recurrent leg trouble in the *Daily Mirror*, **1987**.

Flat racing? No thanks. They're like battery hens – if they don't lay so many eggs they've had their chips.

JENNY PITMAN, the *Independent*.

Etienne Pollet

It was a strange combination. Pat Glennon as dour and as sad as the gloomiest Aussie music-hall comic, spoke no French. Etienne Pollet refused to speak English, although he had an American wife. Whenever there were essential orders, Glennon would stand, looking at the gesticulating French trainer for some minutes. Then he would say in the broadest Strine: 'Shershee Madam Polly.'

TIM FITZGEORGE-PARKER.

Kevin Prendergast

I believe in good oats and good first crop hay. No nuts – nuts are for pigs.

KEVIN PRENDERGAST, **1981**.

We trainers are the most maligned group of people in the world. We find the owners, we employ the staff, we run the stables, we work 365 days a year and we're made to pay for everything. We get nothing free.

KEVIN PRENDERGAST.

My father went mad when I *did* ride in a hurdle race. He said 'If I'd wanted you to be a jump jockey, I would have made you one.'

KEVIN PRENDERGAST.

Paddy Prendergast Sr.

He was one of the worst steeplechase jockeys I've ever known, the other was Noel Murless.

ROGER MORTIMER on Paddy Prendergast.

Sir Mark Prescott

Henry Cecil is a university professor and I'm a comprehensive school teacher.

SIR MARK PRESCOTT, **1981**.

Ryan Price

I've never betted in my life. Never. Why I succeed is because I try *with every single horse*.

RYAN PRICE, *Sunday Express*, **1974**.

Most of my quick decisions have been good ones. After all I met my wife on Sunday and married her on Tuesday.

RYAN PRICE, **1978**.

'Labour will kill racing. Not the Government, not the book-makers, not inflation.' Then he repeated with great emphasis: 'Labour! Mark my words.'

RYAN PRICE, **1979**.

Ryan Price showed me a horse which he said would win at Newton Abbot in two days' time. With a tendon like it had I couldn't see it even getting round. But win it did.

TOM DOWDESWELL, head lad, **1979**.

(*above*) 'It is vulgar to win the Derby two years running' – Lord Weinstock. The Aga Khan did just that with Bahram in 1935 (above) and Mahmoud in 1936. (*below*) 'I was nearly a complete jockey at eighteen but the small gap between what I was then and what I am today took years to fill' – Steve Cauthen. Reference Point and Cauthen storm to victory in the 1987 Derby ahead of Most Welcome and Bellotto

(*above left*) 'His admirers are convinced that had he been at Balaclava he would have kept pace with the Charge of the Light Brigade in precise order and described the riders' injuries before they hit the ground' – Hugh McIlvanney on Peter O'Sullevan. (*above right*) 'People say I look miserable. I don't feel miserable. It's just concentration' – Peter Scudamore. (*below*) 'I don't think I'm brilliant at anything. I'd just sum myself up by saying that I'm very competent' – John Francome, pictured on his way to victory in the King George VI Chase on Burrough Hill Lad

(*above*) 'We soon realized that either Mill Reef was pretty good or the other two-year-olds were useless. As it turned out both were right. He was outstanding and the others were absolutely useless' – Ian Balding. Mill Reef easily beats his rivals in the 1970 Dewhurst Stakes.   (*below*) 'I'm not a natural rider. It has taken very hard work to learn the business' – Willie Carson. The hard work paid off when Carson recorded his first Derby victory in 1979, winning by seven lengths on Troy

(*above left*) 'When I appear in public people expect me to neigh, grind my teeth, paw the ground and swish my tail' – the Princess Royal, pictured at Ascot after winning the Dresden Diamond Stakes on Ten No Trumps.   (*above right*) 'It's one of the real sports that's left to us: a bit of danger and a bit of excitement, and the horses, which are the best thing in the world' – The Queen Mother, enjoying a day at the Derby.   (*below*) 'If I get hold of the man who wrote the rubbish that Burrough Hill Lad would not race again, there is every chance of him being castrated' – Jenny Pitman. Burrough Hill Lad proved the critics wrong when winning the Gold Cup at Cheltenham in 1984

When I stop feelin' shit-scared before an effing selling-plate, I'll effing' give up racing.

RYAN PRICE, quoted by Ivor Herbert, **1979**.

I suppose Ryan Price is the greatest there has ever been with the standard of horse he has had. He has this tremendous rapport with horses.

JACK DOYLE, bloodstock agent, **1982**.

I'm subsidising my owners by £1500 a month. It's true as God is my maker.

RYAN PRICE.

Boy, a little advice for you. Any bloody fool can get to the top of the tree. Don't expect to stay there.

RYAN PRICE's advice to David Barons, **1986**.

Frank Pullen

Frank Pullen, that amazing patcher-up of bad-legged horses, was once kind enough to let me ride a good old selling 'chaser. After weighing in I hurried out to find the trainer.

'Did you buy him back all right?' I asked anxiously and shall never forget Frank's scornful answer.

'Buy him back?' the old trainer said. 'Buy him *back?* Why, when I took the bandages off, they were fainting all round the ring!'

JOHN OAKSEY, on Frank Pullen, *Horse and Hound*.

Eddie Reavey

Bird watching and kicking the wife's cats.

EDDIE REAVEY's entry in the *Directory of the Turf* under 'Recreations', **1980**.

Gordon Richards

When Gordon Richards thinks one of his jockeys has lost a race
he should have won, he is about as reticent as a Hyde Park orator.

GRAHAM ROCK, **1978**.

Mercy Rimell

I don't think I am in favour of women doing the job [of training].
It really takes a man. They handle the labour so much better.

MERCY RIMELL, *Sunday Mirror*, **1971**.

Pat Rohan

We must find more prize money at the lower level if racing is to
continue as we know it today. This will help small trainers and
breeders to continue in business. If we are not careful the strong
will become stronger and the weak could disappear completely.

PAT ROHAN, **1984**.

Mick Ryan

The only things you really need if you want to train are money
and horses, do you know that? Just money and horses because
the Jockey Club don't let you do it unless you've got owners with
money.

MICK RYAN, **1985**.

Ted Smythe

He was strict alright – thorough! Bark worse than his bite though.
He wouldn't have to hit you. He'd give you a coating with his
tongue that would have you in tears.

BRIAN ROUSE on Ted Smythe, to whom he was apprenticed, **1979**.

Major Fred Sneyd

In those days the old man always used to dress for dinner and I used to have to put on a little white coat and serve him sherry and all the rest.

JOE MERCER on Major Fred Sneyd, to whom he was apprenticed, **1979**.

Michael Stoute

I don't blame anyone for retiring a top three-year-old. You've got to look at the equation. The amount of money the horse would earn racing is nothing compared to what he can do at stud.

MICHAEL STOUTE, the *Independent*, **1986**.

Graham Thorner

Racing controls you and if I ever found it didn't want me any more I would get out and try to finish with a clear conscience and no loose ends.

GRAHAM THORNER, *Daily Telegraph*.

Peter Thrale

The reason we Epsom trainers win so many races is that we have no proper gallops.

PETER THRALE.

George Todd

I think it is ridiculous that horses should have to start from stalls in races over one and a half miles.

GEORGE TODD, the *Sun*, **1970**.

He was hard, but my God he made a man of me.

TOMMY CARTER on his former 'guv'nor' George Todd, in *Pacemaker*, **1975**.

Once, a lad looking for a job came into the yard, and seeing George Todd dressed in his smock feeding the horses, mistook him for the head lad. 'They tell me he's a funny man here,' said the lad. 'They say that if you don't do your work properly you don't stay long.' With a wry smile, Todd replied: 'You heard right son.'

COLIN FLEETWOOD-JONES, *Pacemaker*, **1975**.

He lost many a winner out of trying to make a boy a jockey. He'd give them a good lecture but put them up again next time. His orders to an apprentice would always be the same. 'Jump off, get on the fence and stay there. If you don't get out then it's my fault. But you'll be unlucky if an opening doesn't come.'

WALLY MILLS, travelling head lad, on George Todd, **1975**.

Mr Todd was a very heavy better and very rarely left it behind.

WALLY MILLS.

Bob Turnell

Better to be thought a fool than open your mouth and prove it.

BOB TURNELL's advice to his son, trainer Andy Turnell, **1987**.

Bernard van Cutsem

I love horses and I don't think a man should train them if he doesn't.

BERNARD VAN CUTSEM, *Daily Mirror*.

Fulke Walwyn

When I first visited Saxon House as an apprentice amateur, Fulke Walwyn was kind enough to describe my style as 'a good example of the old English lavatory seat.'

JOHN OAKSEY, *Sunday Telegraph*.

Peter Walwyn

If I couldn't train, I'd be unemployable.

PETER WALWYN.

Charlie Whittingham

I'd have won more stakes than any other trainer living – and dead.
At least *those* bastards can't catch me.

CHARLIE WHITTINGHAM, **1980**.

I've had plenty of ups and downs. On one 'down' I went into
tomato farming. Seemed like a good idea. We grew the best
tomatoes. No one wanted 'em. So – back into racing.

CHARLIE WHITTINGHAM.

Norah Wilmot

I sometimes wonder if the powers that be ever feel just a shade
of remorse when they see Miss Wilmot so bravely trying to over-
come the advancing years. Why should her contribution to the
Sport of Kings pass without recognition? That her stable is
patronised by royalty should be sufficient proof of the ability of
a mere woman. If it is considered that a woman would be suscep-
tible to the wiles of scheming men, could the boot not also be on
the other leg? I seem to have heard of a beautiful foreign woman
who got entry into stables controlled by men.

Letter from Mrs Sonia Dingwall to *The Sporting Life*.

Fred Winter

Now, as a trainer, I have one big hate in life – the telephone. My
number rings about 150 times a week and sometimes it nearly
drives me mad. My home is right next door to the yard, so I can
never get away from that side of my life. But really it is my life,
and I don't want it any other way. I go hunting once a year and

I go shooting once a year. I also love golf. But the rest of my life is my horses.

FRED WINTER, the *Sun*.

Fred? Well, he's simply a genius. Funny because I never thought he'd make a good trainer. Ironically, he didn't want to become a trainer – he'd rather have liked to become a Jockey Club starter.

RYAN PRICE on Fred Winter, *The Racehorse*, **1980**.

6
Lads

Wanted, for a sober family, a man of light weight who fears the Lord and can drive a pair of horses. He must occasionally wait at table, join in household prayers, look after the horses, and read a chapter of the Bible.

He must, God willing, rise at seven in the morning, and obey his master and mistress in all commands. If he can dress hair, sing psalms, and play at cribbage, the more agreeable.

N.B. – He must not be familiar with the maidservants, lest the flesh should rebel against the spirit, and he should be introduced to walk in the thorny paths of the wicked. Wages fifteen guineas a year.

Situation vacant, early nineteenth century, advertised in *The Sporting Magazine*.

Never change your place, unless the Lord clearly shows you it is for your soul's good.

Servants Magazine, **1867**.

There is a thing in connection with racing that wants looking into. There is no sort of Fund for the relief of old stablemen, jockeys, etc., except the Bentinck Fund: that is very badly off and the most a man gets is £15 a year which is not enough to keep him out of the work house. I do not suppose that there is another business in the world where the worn-out servants are so badly looked after. I think that with the money that there is in Racing, that some scheme might be started, in which trainers, owners, jockeys and stablemen should have to help to make a Fund – and you are the man to start it.

GEORGE LAMBTON to 17th Lord Derby in **1921**, in *A Classic Connection*.

I naturally appreciate efforts that may be made to improve the lot of anybody associated with the sport of racing, but I honestly cannot give any support to your proposal.

I think that the attempt to form a union is impolitic, and to a certain extent impracticable. It would lead to endless trouble and in some respects would come into conflict with the rules of the Jockey Club.

17TH LORD DERBY in *A Classic Connection*.

The most successful jockeys have been very light smokers; surely that should be an example and a lesson to an ambitious boy. I am strongly of opinion that neither smoking nor drinking should be allowed in the jockeys' dressing rooms, It is such a thoroughly bad example for the younger boys, and the evil of it cannot be exaggerated. The Jockey Club should take the matter in hand. There can be no valid reason against their making some rule to prevent it.

GEORGE LAMBTON in an article in *English Life*, quoted in *A Classic Connection*.

One morning Eph misunderstood his instructions and took his horse on the wrong gallop. The Major was furious and struck Eph two brutal blows with his whip when he returned. Now Eph has been partially deaf from birth and it should have been obvious that he had not heard the orders properly, but the Major was not the man to make allowances for physical disability if he were crossed. The cruel injustice of it sickened me and left me wondering whether my father's misgivings had not been justified.

DOUG SMITH on the treatment of apprentices by Major Fred Sneyd, in *Five Times Champion*.

Stable lads are fools to themselves. They will talk. That's how the bookies get a lot of information.

PAT ROHAN, *Sunday Mirror*.

I think racing's real problem is closer to the horse itself, with the groom or lad who looks after him. Ask anyone directly connected with racing, here or abroad, and they will tell you that the standard of horse care is at its lowest-ever ebb. It makes horses hell to ride, and provides a centre of dissatisfaction at racing's heart. The remedy? Money. Men looking after horses worth £5000 and up are getting £15 a week and some trainers rely on 50 per cent apprentice labour. This is a Dickensian situation deceiving both the lads who are hoping to be jockeys and the owners who are expecting their horses to be looked after by skilled men.

BROUGH SCOTT, 1971.

The death-knell of racing will be labour trouble. You've got to have well-paid, contented staff. You haven't got it. But I got the Benefit Scheme. Who thought of the Jockeys' Saving Plan? I did. Yet, I can't think of one thing I've done which hasn't been opposed by the Jockey Club.

LORD WIGG, 1972.

Spare a thought too for Charlie Potheen's lad, Darkie Deacon. For the Hennessey winner, like Darkie's other charge, The Dickler, is a nightmare ride at home and without the constant help of a strong and fearless horseman, not even Walwyn could have got him ready for yesterday's triumph.

JOHN OAKSEY, *Sunday Telegraph*, 1972.

Although the face is weathered by 10,000 downland mornings . . . the rest of the body is small and almost fraily bird-like. He is only 8st 5lb now, and passed Grade 3 medical for the Army through being underweight and having a skull fracture at the age of twelve.

BROUGH SCOTT on the lad, 'Darkie' Deacon, in *Sunday Times*.

Girl grooms love animals and have a greater feeling for them than men. Kindness in the box makes a great difference to the performance of a horse. A good lad or girl can either make or break a temperamental horse.

JOHN WINTER, *Sunday Telegraph*.

British stable lads are the best in the world.

MR WILFRED SHERMAN, *Daily Telegraph*.

I wish occasionally the stewards would go round the stable lads'
quarters and see for themselves. The stewards live in the luxury
of free meals, free drinks, and comfortable seats provided by the
management and it would not be proper to upset this status quo.
But it has got to be upset if racing is to keep its diminishing labour
force.

RICHARD BAERLEIN, 1973.

There's a favourite story that's told in America about a groom
working in a racing stable. One day he went to see the trainer
and gave in his notice. Asked why, the groom replied: 'On account
of the trickle-down.' 'The trickle down. What's that?' was the
bewildered trainer's response. 'It's lots o' money comin' at the
top, but not much tricklin' down to me,' came the answer.

Pacemaker editorial, 1974.

My heart is still in racing and I still find time to ride out occasionally for one or two trainers. But I can't face going back as a stable
lad. I'd rather get out of the game. You work all the hours in the
week for so little money. As a postman I can earn much more
and I have plenty of free time. This summer I'm taking my wife
on our first holiday since I came into racing more than eight years
ago.

JOCK WILKINSON, *Sunday People*, 1974.

Dinner was a single slice of stale bread and marg., with jam on
Tuesdays and Thursdays. There were two to a bed, no holidays,
even at Christmas and the Long Tom for offenders. They were
paid nothing at all for the first three years and half a crown a
week thereafter.

JIMMY WHITE, on his days as an apprentice, *The Times*.

Apart from meagre pay and rough living, their biggest frustration
is that which motivates most revolts in the end: the sense that an
all powerful authority pays only lip service to their grievances.
The trainer is seen as the adjutant, the owner as some visiting
colonel-in-chief and the Jockey Club as a High Command somewhat remoter and less sensitive to their tiresome problems than
the War Office is to the average squaddie.

IAN WOOLDRIDGE on the Newmarket strike, *Daily Mail*, 1975.

We can't pay stable staff more unless we charge owners more. And if we charge owners more, many will take their horses away, making many stable lads redundant.

JOHN WINTER, **1975**.

There is a great shortage of top class talent. Why? Because trainers can't be bothered with them.

DAVID NICHOLSON on apprentices, the *Sun*.

Present-day apprentices get too much too easily. They don't know what it's like to live on bread and butter, but all the best jockeys have come up the hard way.

PETER ROBINSON, *Racing World*, **1977**.

First take careful note of the lad leading the horse round the parade ring. If he keeps glancing up at the creature, it is possible that he has backed it himself and that it has a chance. When the lad, and the horse for that matter, march glumly around looking nowhere, you can be sure that's where they're going that afternoon.

ROBERT MORLEY, actor.

It is the stable lads I feel sorry for when I see those huge sales prices. What must they think? They are left in charge of priceless stock and yet people are still haggling over a minimum wage for them.

CHARLES ST GEORGE, **1977**.

Introducing a minimum wage would be like telling Jeremy [Tree] how much to pay his butler.

SIR RANDLE FEILDEN, **1977**.

The wages for a 'full lad' when he had done his time were £2 weekly. We are talking not of the Victorian age, but of fifty years ago. Holidays? There were no bloomin' holidays. If you asked for a day off you might as well have given in your notice. I'd no choice. What else could I do and live? There were millions out of work. Then if you didn't work you bloody starved. . . . So your boss could sack you on the spot, right there, if you so much as answered him back. It was like being in prison, really.

BOB TURNELL, *Sunday Express*, **1977**.

I grumble a bit about staff. I know I probably shouldn't but I think back how I was brought up in stables. They get away with murder today.

HARRY WRAGG, **1978**.

The case for more prize money has been put far too high . . . We found the argument for increased prize money as a remedy for the low wages of staff particularly unconvincing. . . . We think that increased wages should come from higher training fees.

ROYAL COMMISSION ON GAMBLING, **1978**.

I know of instances where a lad has actually worked seventeen hours in a day – without being paid overtime, travelling a horse to a distant meeting. And while feeding his charge well, he had to go hungry himself because his £2 allowance was enough only to buy one decent meal in a motorway café.

TOMMY DELANEY, Stable Lads Association, **1978**.

Can a writer seriously expect racing folk to regard what has become known as the Last Charge of the Blimps as a splendid occasion? It was the most hideous display of social and industrial prejudice ever my displeasure to witness.

CHRISTOPHER POOLE on the 'Battle of the Rowley Mile', *Evening Standard*, **1978**.

'Pat, there's one golden rule in this yard. I don't want you taking any women upstairs.'

'Okay, guv'nor,' said the lad, and promptly went upstairs and dragged the mattress down to the ground floor.

JEFFREY BERNARD.

I didn't care if it was a bad horse or a good one. They all got the same treatment from me – love and affection. It's just that I remember the good ones a little bit better.

TOM DOWDESWELL, **1979**.

In my day an apprentice did one horse until he managed to do it right, then he did two. Now they have to do three or four – there is no way it can be done properly.

TOM DOWDESWELL.

They are all owned by other people, but to me they are *my* horses and I love them.

PADDY RUDKIN, head lad to Henry Cecil, **1979**.

In the material improvements brought in racing since the war, the welfare of the racehorse and of those who look after him have enjoyed a low priority. Stands have been built for astronomical prices, yet the amenities for horses and stable lads have often remained the same for the past 50 years. At one course where a fortune was spent on grandstands, the lads were still lodged in Army huts left over from the 1914–18 war.

The British Racehorse, **1979**.

There is no way that I could have Diamond Edge race-fit but for the application and dedication of my stable lads. They came willingly back to the yard every afternoon in the hope that we could work.

FULKE WALWYN, *Daily Mail*, **1979**.

I am certain that far too many people take their labour force for granted. Without caring for them we are all in the cart.

JOHN DUNLOP, quoted by Brough Scott in the *Sunday Times*, **1980**.

It is now as clear as daylight that something must be done to help these lads. It is wrong that trainers should take half a fee from a boy. The lad's entitled to the lot. Trainers are putting up moderate lads just to pocket the cash. If this anomaly were removed then trainers would only put up lads who were worth their fee.

BOB TURNELL on the Conditional Jockey Scheme, which gave inexperienced riders more opportunities, **1980**.

It is no good if you cannot talk with the lads. They are closer to the horses than you and a good one can tell you as much as your own eyes any day, if not more.

FULKE WALWYN, *Sunday Telegraph*.

Fred Flippance [head lad] taught me all the groundwork I know. Legwork and everything else came from Fred and it was a great sadness that he died so young.

ALEC STEWART, **1986**.

There are a hell of a lot of lads who would dearly love to join the Stable Lads Association but are a bit frightened for their jobs, particularly in small yards.

BILL ADAMS, secretary of Stable Lads Association, **1986**.

A lot of non-caring trainers won't pay their staff the minimum wage.

BILL ADAMS, letter to *The Sporting Life*, **1986**.

At last we have got the trainers in a corner.

BILL ADAMS, **1987**.

Henry Cecil's particular strength is the time he spends with his horses and his staff, and his affection for them all. His yard is a surprising world apart from those grim concentration camps which were Newmarket stables twenty years ago. Then apprentices stood quivering to attention, showing their laid-out grooming kits, and squeaking out 'Sir' to despotic trainers.

IVOR HERBERT, *Mail on Sunday*, **1987**.

Some handouts are traditional, amounts are eagerly discussed in advance, and comparisons made both before and after the event. Imagine then, the creeping horror with which one stable lad watched as a particular lord patted the horse, put his hand in his pocket, drew out a sugar lump, gave it to the horse . . . and turned to go. The lad was so stunned, he couldn't stop himself from tugging heavily on his cap and saying,

'Excuse me, your Lordship.'

'Yes?'

'Er, well,' said the lad, giving the peak of his cap another pull; by now the top half of his face had disappeared, but distress registered plainly on the lower regions.

'Yes?' said his Lordship. 'What is it?'

'Well,' stumbled the lad, 'it's just that . . . what shall I tell the other lads you gave me?'

From *Bedside Racing*.

Only on Friday, a twenty-year-old Lancashire lad told me how he joined a Midland stable last spring to find that he, another apprentice and a sixteen-year-old non-riding school leaver were the only staff to look after eighteen horses. All three slept in the same room, two in the same bed, and throughout his four months stay his gross wages were kept at least £20 below the national agreed minimum.

BROUGH SCOTT, *Sunday Times*.

Forget the Cossacks and the Comanches; the greatest horsemen in the world are the Newmarket stable lads.

SUSAN GALLIER, stable girl to Clive Brittain, in *One of the Lads*, **1988**.

If there's one thing a stable lad has, which no trainer or owner or racing tycoon can buy or take away from him, then it's the personal relationships he shares with his horses.

SUSAN GALLIER.

7

Racecourses

A Welsh farmer called before the stewards to give evidence after the last race, protested vigorously at the inconvenience. The presiding steward tried to calm him down by pointing out that on occasions even the running of the Queen's horses had been the subject of inquiry.

'I dare say,' said the farmer, far from appeased, 'but when Her Majesty gets home she doesn't have to milk fifty cows.'

ANON.

The other day there was a very old chap with a stick, coming out of the Haydock members' exit. At that moment another equally old racegoer came round the corner, tripped over the stick and fell down. Looking up he saw the man who was with him and shouted in a broad Lancastrian voice. 'Take his name, ref!' I thought Matt Busby would never stop laughing!

JOHN HUGHES, **1974**.

I'm not sure I'm happy for racecourses to be owned by book-makers – there could be grounds for a conflict of interests.

SIR DESMOND (now Lord) PLUMMER, **1975**.

I think you could probably reduce the sixty-six racecourses to something like fifty without doing a great deal of harm.

LORD HOWARD DE WALDEN, **1977**.

I am inclined to think that those who buy food on a racecourse, except from dire necessity, ought to have their heads carefully examined at an early opportunity by a really good man.

ROGER MORTIMER, *The Racehorse*, **1977**.

The watering system has yet to be devised that is as good as that produced by the Almighty.

JOHN SANDERSON, clerk of the course at York.

We must reduce the number of racecourses in Britain. It's our only hope (not) to go to the gallows and preserve our better tracks. We need to lose approximately 100 of the 984 fixtures and this means lopping a few courses.

SIR DESMOND PLUMMER, chairman of the Betting Levy Board, **1979**

When I hear that the same set of architects who built the new stands at Doncaster and those at Leopardstown were to build the new stands at Goodwood my heart sank. Although Doncaster is better that the latest monstrosity at Cheltenham, it should have been vastly improved by a study beforehand of some of the best stands in the world including those at Flemington, Melbourne and Singapore.

RICHARD BAERLEIN, the *Observer*, **1979**.

You can tread on that turf and the rabbits wouldn't hear you come. It's velvet.

MICHAEL PHILLIPS, racing correspondent of *The Times*, on the Lambourn gallops, *Pacemaker*, **1980**.

I do say for the umpteenth time that the water jump is a pointless, needlessly dangerous fence, which even in its emasculated form, can become a hidden trap for the kind of horse we can least afford to lose.

JOHN OAKSEY, *Horse and Hound*, **1981**.

This may not be a recognized training area, but we're not training around the pits.

STEVE NORTON on his Barnsley stables, **1981**.

I wouldn't go to any racecourse if I wasn't riding.

WILLIE CARSON, **1982**.

Levy money spent on new grandstands is money squandered. It's like building hotels with bedrooms which will never be let.

IVOR HERBERT, *Mail on Sunday*, **1982**.

The problems are always to do with staff. If the girls are smiling and jolly, people feel happy, but if you get a surly old boot behind the bar. . . .

TIM NELIGAN, managing director of United Racecourses, on catering, **1984**.

It is a disgrace. Here we are in 1984 and concrete posts are still being used. What on earth would happen if some one's spine was wrapped round one? The boy was lucky to get away with a broken leg and I think it's criminal.

PAUL COLE, on an accident to jockey Steve Dawson, **1984**.

If a jockey is thrown into contact with one of these there is not much point in holding a stewards' inquiry because the whole thing will have to be retold in a Coroner's Court . . . If the Board leaves one concrete post in the ground it will stand as a memorial to wrong-thinking, wrong-values – and a completely cynical attitude that puts money before the lives of those who provide us with brilliant sport.

MONTY COURT, The *Weekender*, **1986**.

No intoxicating liquor may be taken into the jockeys' dressing-room.

Sign outside the weighing-room at Downpatrick.

I have seen people taking in crates of beer and then using them as seats round the paddock.

LORD FAIRHAVEN, senior steward of the Jockey Club, **1986**.

The scrunch of those flimsy plastic mugs has become an all too familiar sound on the British racecourse.

LORD FAIRHAVEN.

I cannot understand why the introduction of all-weather racing is proving such a problem. If all other countries in the world can do it, I don't see why we are making such a fuss.

TIM NELIGAN, managing director of United Racecourses, **1987**.

I hope this doesn't turn out to be just another hoax.

The commentator on Irish television, talking about the 50-minute delay of the start of the Irish Derby at the Curragh because of a bomb scare, **1987**.

Racing is really an alfresco drinking club that moves its location from day to day.

JEFFREY BARNARD.

Aintree

Foinavon has no chance. Not the boldest of jumpers, he can be safely ignored, even in a race noted for shocks.

CHARLES BENSON, *Daily Express*, **1967**. Foinavon won.

I love the Liverpool course. The National is part and parcel of everything British, and racing without it just doesn't seem possible. Where else in the world do you get a spectacle like it? Thirty horses fanning out over those big, black fences. Surely this is what the game is all about. Perhaps I've been brainwashed by it all. For me, Liverpool has everything; Cheltenham has nothing. To hell with the prestige of winning at Cheltenham. I don't like the place and you don't get the same appreciation of a good horse in the South that you get here in the North.

GINGER MCCAIN, *Sunday Mirror*, **1973**.

One day, describing the scene in the Aintree paddock on television, Clive said. 'That large figure in the centre is local steward,

the Earl of Sefton, who nearly suffered a very nasty motor accident in London on his way to Liverpool this morning.'

There was the devil to pay. Lord Sefton's home, Croxteth, was
bombarded with telephone calls from anxious friends and relations
who wanted to know if he was alright. 'He was hopping mad with
me the next day,' said Clive. 'But I told him it was entirely his
own fault and that he should learn in future not to stop on an
amber traffic light. He was jolly lucky that I didn't run into the
back of him!'

TIM FITZGEORGE-PARKER on Clive Graham – The Scout, **1974**.

The Grand National itself is an anachronism. It was a marvellous
race when there was no lack of great big Irish-bred horses standing
over 16 hands and capable of carrying a 13st man across Leicester-
shire. Very often horses of that sort never raced until they were
four or jumped a fence until they were six.

ROGER MORTIMER, *The Racehorse*, **1980**.

The attitude of the Turf authorities to Aintree in recent years has
been one of sustained, unvarying hypocrisy.

Timeform's Chasers & Hurdlers, **1980/81**.

How much would be involved to secure the future of Aintree as
the venue for the Grand National – to purchase the course and
bring its spartan and ramshackle amenities up to modern standards? Say ten million, although some would argue this is on the
high side.

To put the sum in perspective, it is worth pointing out that the
loans to Goodwood, Haydock and Cheltenham alone will probably cost the Levy Board around one hundred million pounds in
compound interest.

Timeform's Chasers & Hurdlers 1980/81, in the comment on Aldaniti.

Now that the aristocratic Jockey Club have at last done a deal,
they are patting themselves on the back, but it was one of their
own members, the late Lord Sefton, who started the whole farce.
He was one of the richest men in the land but sold the course to
Mrs Topham purely for financial gain.

CLAUDE DUVAL, the *Sun*, **1982**.

Perhaps the installation of Lord Vestey as chairman of the extra-
vagantly titled Grand National Campaign may have bred a touch
of cynicism. With the greatest respect to his lordship, a man who
has satisfactorily settled several taxing problems in the past, there
is something a trifle incongruous in the sight of a mountainously
rich man rattling a begging bowl. It may have occurred to one or
two innocent souls that the noble lord could have spared us the
entire circus – campaigns, professional fund-raisers and the like –
by organizing a discreet whip-round among a few of his chums,
since Jockey Club paupers are notoriously thin on the ground.

PATRICK COLLINS, *Daily Mail*, **1982**.

No one can throw a stone at Ladbrokes! Over our seven years
managing the Grand National we've spent £3½ million. Without
us Aintree would now be a car park.

RON POLLARD, managing director of Ladbrokes, **1983**.

Aintree used to terrify me. The first time, I walked the course
alone. The only thought that kept me there was that other human
beings had jumped it. And they'd been doing it for quite a while.

After I won last year, I went back to the course. They'd stripped
the fences; and just the blackthorn was growing. There was so
much peace. Birds nesting in the fences and rabbits scampering
around. I wanted to parcel it up as my other memory of Aintree.
Just the skeleton of the thing that frightened me so much.

EDDIE HARTY, who won the **1974** Grand National on Highland Wedding.

The last few moments before the off I always think: 'I wish to
God it was tomorrow.'

EDDIE HARTY, on the Grand National, **1975**.

I would never track horses that were making mistakes. I hadn't
got enough light at the Chair on Highland Wedding. And I said:
'Please God, send me a little light' – and suddenly it opened up.

EDDIE HARTY, **1975**.

If it were just racing, you'd know very early on whether you had a chance. But Aintree is special. You keep going because you know there could be a fall. Bridles have broken. Horses have had heart seizures. Men have got cricks in their necks. They've even gone on the wrong course.

EDDIE HARTY.

After Becher's, the next one feels like the smallest on the course. But that's where the big pile-up happened in 1967 – Foinavon's year. I saw it coming. They went down like a pack of cards in front of me. And I thought: 'I've won the National.'

But you can't afford the luxury of excitement. The horse refused and I fell off like a kid at a gymkhana.

EDDIE HARTY.

I did not take Aintree over because I saw the chance of making quick money – I could have done better deals in a strict financial sense. I bought Aintree to save a race which belongs to the British public, which is unique and has 140 years of tradition behind it.

BILL DAVIES, property developer, **1975**.

I can't tell you the feeling winning the race gives you. I think I cried, then laughed, then cried again. You are on the crest of a wave.

JOHN PRICE, Toby Balding's travelling head lad on winning the **1974** Grand National with Highland Wedding.

On reflection I'm sorry I hit him at all. For the rest of my life I've got to live with the fact that I threw away the Grand National with that one error.

RICHARD PITMAN, rider of Crisp, **1978**.

The race means so much more to me because I did not win it.

RICHARD PITMAN, on the Grand National after his retirement, **1978**.

The race, the place, means so much to my life that my ambition is to be associated with a National winner, either as an owner or trainer. It remains the ultimate challenge for me.

RICHARD PITMAN.

It wasn't a great day for seeing . . . you could see three or four fences – no more. I can't remember too much about the race except that he went through a hole in the last and gave me a fright! Yes, that was the greatest day of my life. I didn't get home for a week.

EDDIE DEMPSEY, rider of 100–1 **1947** Grand National winner Caughoo, who was widely rumoured not to have completed the full course in the fog.

Believe me, despite the bravado, we all really knew fear in the olden days. We all said a little prayer before we went down to post. . . .

JOHNNY BULLOCK, who rode Nickel Coin to victory in **1951** in the Grand National.

McCain always maintained that Dempsey hid under the Canal Turn and only went round the once. There was a proper battle about it one night outside a pub.

JACK DOYLE, on the riders of the first and second in the **1946** Grand National.

It serves no purpose, and I find it somewhat obscene.

TONY MORRIS on the Grand National, **1983**.

It was great. It's the greatest achievement a jump jockey can have. It's always what you wanted ever since you first started riding. I am only sorry I never won it twice.

WILLIE ROBINSON on winning the Grand National on Team Spirit in **1964**.

People tend to think that it takes a horse with great guts to win the National. They are wrong. Rubstic was the most gutless horse I have ever come across. He jumped because he was frightened to death of hurting himself in a fall. He won because he was clever.

JOHN LEADBEATER, trainer of the **1979** Grand National winner.

Two days after she won the National the press wanted a picture of Sheila's Cottage, and Arthur Thompson was putting on the bridle when the old bitch bit off the top of his finger. I wanted Arthur to see the doctor, but he was as tough as her. He jumped on the mare's back and the photographer got his picture.

NEVILLE CRUMP, 1985.

Sheila's Cottage was going well for Arthur Thompson, and I was beginning to feel we might win. I turned to John Proctor, her owner, expecting him to be roaring his horse home. Instead he was polishing off the remains of a flask of brandy. 'Look here, aren't you interested?' I asked. 'We could be winning the bloody National, you know.' John looked quite unconcerned and replied: 'Neville, you look after the horses and I'll see to the drinks!'

NEVILLE CRUMP.

If he were mine, I wouldn't run a horse in the National with more than twelve stone.

JENNY PITMAN, 1985.

In the past twenty years there have been 272 fallers in the Grand National excluding horses which were brought down or unseated their riders – of which sixty-eight (twenty-five per cent) have occurred at Bechers. Of the ten killed during the same period Becher's has claimed four victims.

MICHAEL SEELY, *The Times*, 1987.

I am converted to the view that Becher's Brook is an unfair obstacle which can and should be modified.

JOHN OAKSEY, 1987.

Ascot

There will be steeplechasing at Ascot only over my dead body.

BERNARD, DUKE OF NORFOLK, speaking before steeplechasing was introduced in 1965.

Jumping at Ascot is like Blackpool with the tide out.

JOHN HISLOP, *The Wit of the Turf.*

At one time a little humdrum adultery could prove a barrier to the Royal Enclosure, but now something rather more spectacular is required, such as hi-jacking a Securicor van or taking too prominent a role in a sex instruction film designed for circulation in the best preparatory schools.

ROGER MORTIMER, *Sunday Times*, **1971**.

Applying for membership of the Members' Stand at Ascot is now on a par with applying for a passport. One must have the application approved by one of the following list: Ascot annual member, member of the Jockey Club, Justice of the Peace, Minister of Religion, Medical Practitioner, Bank Manager, Chief Constable, Assistant Chief Constable, Barrister or Solicitor. It is a wide choice provided one is not an atheist, bankrupt, sick, or in trouble with the law.

RICHARD BAERLEIN, **1971**.

You don't want just anyone coming into your club. Over my dead body will I see the Private Stand at Ascot opened up to anyone who can pay.

THE LATE DUKE OF NORFOLK, **1975**.

When I die I want it to be on Ascot Gold Cup Day.

BETTY KENWOOD, 'Jennifer' from *Harpers & Queen*, in **1979**.

Earlier on this year I was invited to Ascot, and looked around and thought: 'How can the country survive this bloody lot?' I felt guilty being there – that I ought to be working – the mess we're in as a country and all this lot prancing around. By hell, I thought, the sooner you get back to Brum the better.

A Tory managing director, *Sunday Telegraph*, **1979**.

Queen Mary ordered a sporty peeress to be removed from the

Royal Enclosure at Ascot because she wore a round sailor cap with 'HMS Good Ship Venus' in gold lettering.

KENNETH ROSE, *Sunday Telegraph*, **1982**.

Apart from the still gloriously groomed Royal Drive down the course, Ascot, in the last five years, had slumped from a 'My Fair Lady' spectacle into a vulgar and tatty farce.

JEAN ROOK, *Daily Express*, **1983**

Cartmel

You haven't been racing if you haven't been to Cartmel. And I mean it.

JONJO O'NEILL, *Daily Mirror*.

In 1860 a sweepstake took place over a distance of ten furlongs between two horses called Woodmite and Creeper. There were no less than ten false starts before the race commenced, but then on pulling up the rider of Creeper, who finished second, claimed that they had been round the course twice instead of three times, so promptly remounted, went round again, and claimed the twenty-five sovereigns prize. After 'a good deal of dispute', stakes were divided.

MARTEN JULIAN recalling an historic moment at Cartmel, **1982**.

Chantilly

None of their turf gallops had the deep-rooted old turf like you find at Newmarket, Manton or Russley. The only place where you nearly get it is on the racecourse where you can work on the middle or outside of the course itself. Why do you think trainers get up at 4.30 in the morning to try and beat each other to the gallops? They do it to try to be the first on them and get the best of the ground.

WALTER SWINBURN SENIOR on Chantilly, **1975**.

Take one measure of Goodwood, two of Salisbury, add a dash of

Château setting and you have a cocktail called Chantilly, and on a cold damp day last Sunday I left the racecourse shaken but not stirred.

PRINCE 'PIPPI', **1978**.

Cheltenham

It is scarcely possible to turn our steps in any direction without hearing the voice of the blasphemous, or meeting the reeling drunkard, or witnessing scenes of the lowest profligacy.

THE REV. F.C. (DEAN) CLOSE on the **1827** Cheltenham race week.

IRISH RACEGOER at Cheltenham: 'I was so excited when Arkle won that I lost my teeth.'
ENGLISH RACEGOER: 'I know a trainer at Lambourn who is still wearing them.'

One of Cheltenham's most famous, or infamous, characters, was Black Tom Oliver. Black Tom, so-called because of his swarthy skin and disordered style of dress, was much respected as a horseman and revered as a man, yet lived and died in constant debt. Many tales remain of his brushes with the law and according to the *Cheltenham Mercury* on one occasion he fooled the sheriff's bailiffs, who had surrounded the public house where he was hiding, by escaping in the coffin of a recently-deceased employee. The landlord's connivance in this flouting of the law is explained by the fact that he part-owned the horse Tom was off to ride – it duly won.

JULIETTE HARRISON, **1974**.

Never. It's an appalling thought.

LORD WILLOUGHBY DE BROKE on building a Flat racecourse at Cheltenham, **1977**.

We could have the finest eighteen hole course in the West country.

LORD WILLOUGHBY DE BROKE on Cheltenham, **1977**.

I have this recurring bad dream of the interminable two-mile chase which goes on for ever because the dolls haven't been moved.

PHILIP ARKWRIGHT, clerk of the course at Cheltenham, **1978**.

I find it fairly sickening to reflect that one has to be a rugby player of almost international standard to get to the bars.

JEFFREY BERNARD on Cheltenham, **1979**.

But I still have one good memory of Cheltenham to cling on to. That was the time when Fred Winter won on Sky Pink. Twenty runners, almost last over the final flight, and then won going away at 100 to 8. It's the only time I've ever had the shape of a suit ruined by the bulk of the pound notes.

JEFFREY BERNARD.

I rode Cheltenham like this. First you must get a close up position before the water jump. This is vital. Then you can hold that position sitting into him nicely on the bridle up the hill past Frenchie's place to that ditch on the top. If you are pushing there, off the bridle, you are in trouble and then, as Lord Mildmay used to say, that can be the worst fence in England, even if he has got his second wind.

Now you can give him a breather, free wheel down the hill. But you must have your race won at the second last. You must ride for that. The second last has almost always been my winning post. If you haven't won at the second last, you are not going to win anyway. From here you have two options. If you are going well enough, you can give him a breather around that bend before wriggling into the last and home. Or you can ride like hell into the last and all the way up the hill to the winning post.

Funny thing. That Cheltenham hill they all talk about. I never found it anything like as steep as some courses – Sandown, Carlisle for instance. If you were right at the second last, the hill was no bother.

TIM MOLONY, quoted by Tim Fitzgeorge-Parker, **1979**.

Cheltenham's new million-plus stand is surely an improvement but if you have binoculars capable of seeing through concrete pillars, you're advised to bring them.

PETER O'SULLEVAN, **1979**.

Doncaster

Do you know what goes on in Doncaster during the great race-week in early September? Importation of scores of prostitutes, immigration of scores of practical thieves, thimble-riggers, pick-pockets, gamblers and cheats of every description, liquor shops open at night, houses of ill-fame all open, drinking, cursing, swearing and fighting; in plain words 'Hell broke loose in the slums of Doncaster'.

A vicar's view of the Tower Moors in the nineteenth century, from *The Fast Set.*

Epsom

In handing over the gallops, I have in mind what the people of England have given to the Wootton family.

STANLEY WOOTTON, **1970**.

I stood up there and I looked over the marvellous hill and over the trees on Walton Downs and there was Headley Church standing up against the sky; and I thought 'Why not for ever?' and by God we've done it.

GEORGE WIGG, who with Stanley Wootton saved The Derby.

And Epsom! It's the queerest course I've ever ridden on. It's not just the hill but the angle. I never expected to see anything like that. And to think you run the greatest race in the world on it. I feel most trainers back home would take one look at it and put their horses right back in the box!

MICK GOREHAM, Australian jockey, **1974**.

On the train to Tattenham Corner there was the usual sense of wonder about the willingness of so many people to settle for being somewhere other than Epsom on this afternoon. Glimpses of men hoeing vegetable patches, of women hanging out clothes, or of clerks and executives in dark suits steering briefcases through sweating crowds at East Croydon, evoked a strange, presumptuous sympathy. The physical reality of the Derby is so magical for some of us that we are inclined to feel sorry for anyone who misses out on it. We find it hard to accept that there are millions who are happy to take a less intimate, more ephemeral pleasure from the event, for whom the Derby is a momentary thrill, a fleeting blur of excitement that brightens a working week, a parade watched from office or factory window.

HUGH MCILVANNEY, **1975**.

God knows, you've got no chance with a race like the Derby. The bastards are all trying.

A head lad, quoted by JEFFREY BERNARD, **1979**.

The Derby is a national day out for aristocrats and artisans, gypsies and generals, viscounts and villains.

TIM NELIGAN, managing director of United Racecourses, **1979**.

It has always been a mystery to me why our best race should be run on our worst racecourse.

JULIAN WILSON on Epsom, BBC TV.

Goodwood

The King had a lavatory in statuary marble with his monogram, a double-thickness mahogany seat, and a marble frieze and skirting. All the metal work was silver-plated, including the door hinges and the flushing handle. Goodwood might be going popular, but it did not intend to ignore the niceties of life.

From *Goodwood*.

As the event becomes a little more 'popular' and as more private boxes come to be taken by businessmen, the more elite-conscious begin to feel uneasily that their uniqueness is being challenged and drift away. It becomes smarter to miss Ascot and go to the smaller meeting at Goodwood where it is fashionable *not* to dress up.

From *The Aristocrats*.

Happy Valley (Hong Kong)

An English lady once likened the sight of a crowd leaving Happy Valley Racecourse to blackcurrants going through a sieve.

MICHAEL HARRIS, *Pacemaker*, **1978**.

Newmarket

Goodbye, God bless you, my Newmarket lads.

DANIEL DAWSON, horse poisoner, on the eve of his hanging on 8 August **1812**.

Efficiency is of a high order and the milk of human kindness runs very thin indeed. . . . Throughout the land the British class system has gone to pot. Daughters of duchesses marry sons of dustmen with a flourish. The leader of the Conservative Party went to a grammar school and at Cheltenham the Queen Mother shook hands with a bookmaker's clerk who had a cigarette in his mouth . . . but at racing's headquarters the feudal system is strong.

CLEMENT FREUD on Newmarket, the *Sun*, **1968**.

There's no place like Newmarket for making a horse sour. All those wide open spaces . . . how boring. I've just had one come up from there who gets to the gallop and won't budge. He just stands still – a legacy of queueing up at Newmarket, I suppose.

MICK EASTERBY, talking to Phil Rostran in *Pacemaker*.

Racing at Newmarket is something of an acquired taste.

ROGER MORTIMER, *Sunday Times*.

By and large the opening day of the Craven Meeting at Newmarket was nicely suited to elderly racegoers who have been advised by their doctors to avoid if possible any danger of undue excitement.

ROGER MORTIMER, *The Racehorse*, **1976**.

You get the impression that nothing else but racing matters there.

PETER WILLETT, on Newmarket, **1979**.

Siberia.

PAUL KELLEWAY on Newmarket in winter, **1983**.

Not for nothing has the Cesarewitch been described as hanging about in Suffolk for a race that is run in Cambridgeshire.

ROGER MORTIMER, **1983**.

Newmarket is diabolical. What's the point of races where the public can see only a fraction of what's going on? This is supposed to be a spectator sport.

JOHN SHARRATT, race-reader, **1985**.

8

Horses

I speak Spanish to God, Italian to women, French to men and German to my horse.

EMPEROR CHARLES V (**1500–1558**).

Men are not hanged for stealing horses, but that horses may not be stolen.

MARQUIS OF HALIFAX (**1633–1695**).

I have lost my mistress, horse, and wife,
And when I think of human life,
Cry mercy 'twas no worse.
My mistress sickly, poor and old,
My wife dam'd ugly and a scold, -
I am sorry for my horse.

ANON (eighteenth-century epigrams).

Fancy a great sixteen 'and 'oss lyin' on one like a blanket, or sittin' with his monstrous hemispheres on one's chest; sending one's werry soul out o' one's nostrils. Dreadful thought. Vere's the brandy?

MR JORROCKS.

I feel sure that horses are every bit as clever as dogs, and if they could live in the house and be always with one there would not be much to choose between them in the way of faithfulness and intelligence. The Arabs have proved this by treating their horses as friends and companions far more than we do in this country.

MARGUERITE DE BEAUMONT in *The Way of a Horse*.

Men are generally more careful of the breed of their horses and dogs than of their children.

WILLIAM PENN in *Fruits of Solitude*.

A real racehorse should have a head like a lady and a behind like a cook.

JACK LEACH.

They come into the world basically decent – it's just a matter of seeing that they don't go wrong.

SIR NOEL MURLESS, the *Daily Mail*.

Most sheep are more stupid than most horses. I have yet to meet a cow that could pass 'O' levels. And even horses are not stupid enough to bet on men. But they aren't intellectually bright.

NOEL WHITCOMB, the *Sun*.

The welfare of the horse himself is one of the most important features of racing, yet it is steadily being pushed aside.

JOHN HISLOP, *British Racehorse*, **1969**.

I am reminded of an old cavalry maxim: 'Horses first, men second, officers last'. It might be applied equally well to racing as I would wish to see it – the racehorse itself first, the men second, and owners last.

T. E. WATSON, *The Racehorse*, **1970**.

All great horses are easy to shoe.

JOHN FFRENCH, farrier of Lambourn, in *Sunday Times*.

Whenever a horse's racing career has come to an end, Auriol Sinclair has the animal put down in her own yard when possible. 'I hold them myself, and at least I know where they have ended up.'

From a PAT LUCAS profile, *Horse and Hound*, **1972**.

It was the plainest Oaks field I have ever seen, and the paddock critic who expressed a decided preference for the horse of the policewoman on duty was no bad judge.

ROGER MORTIMER, *Sunday Times*, **1972**.

I am starting a society for the abolition of horses. They are useless animals and should be kept in National Parks as biological freaks. Consider the horse. His stupidity is unparalleled in nature; he does nothing but eat and sleep. He cannot jump higher than a man; his droppings are full of grass and useless. He produces nothing, unlike the cow which gives us milk and manure which is worth its weight in gold. In agriculture, his place has been taken by the tractor; he gives many people hay fever, including myself. He doesn't come when he is called. He is a most frightful bore. In short, his only usefulness to my way of thinking is to delay a girl's awareness of boys, thus keeping the population down.

LORD ARRAN, *Evening News*.

The great thing with horses is to have an open mind. Don't prejudge them, for there's always something to like in any horse even though it's sometimes hard to find.

CLIVE BRITTAIN, *Stud and Stable*.

I concentrate on the minds of horses and try to understand them. There is always a reason for their behaviour. We try to keep them interested by playing pop music from the radio every morning in the yard. Horses are like children. They respond, particularly to kindness.

FRANK MUGGERIDGE, *News of the World*.

Racehorses, like women, are entirely unpredictable.

RICHARD BAERLEIN, the *Observer*.

I regard horses as cunning creatures and they have got to be mastered. I treat a racehorse as a machine. To get the best service from a machine you treat it carefully. It is the same with racehorses. Father has taught me that if you make a pet of a racehorse it will go soft and silly and will not win races.

LESTER PIGGOTT.

Under no circumstances should any aged horse belonging to me be sold, but that my usual custom be observed with regard to having such horse humanely put down by my stable veterinary surgeon on the premises.

GEORGE TODD's Will, **1974**.

Horses in big race stables lead an unnatural life.

MRS LOUISE DINGWALL, trainer.

Firing causes the horse totally unnecessary pain. If one of ours breaks down, the missus puts its leg in plaster of Paris for six weeks, then we use a blister – our own special recipe which has been handed down through the family for generations.

DAVID NICHOLSON, *The Sporting Life,* **1975**.

The eye of a sick horse can tell you all you need to know about him.

SYD MERCER, *Sunday Telegraph*.

Horseflesh is an international currency. It is an asset you can always shift. Unlike having property in England, say, that you can't move, you can shift a horse. If you have a Derby winner you will get bids from America, Australia, Japan. It is a very international commodity.

ROBERT SANGSTER, **1977**.

The suggestion that the weights should be raised again is a bad one. The modern thoroughbred, in general, is a weaker animal than his forebears, who walked miles to and from stations before every race, and is not capable of carrying bigger burdens.

TIM FITZGEORGE-PARKER, **1977**.

When a horse comes to me I give him all the love there is in my heart. After all we only pass this way but once.

LOUISE DINGWALL.

The average merit of two-year-olds should be about the same each year. It is impossible to have two-year-olds as bad as they have been assessed this year.

REG GRIFFIN, managing director of *Timeform*, on the international classification for two-year-olds, **1979**.

In recent years Stalbridge Colonist, Don't Hesitate and Bachelor's Hall have all broken down because they were forced to hump 12 stone. You are pandering to bad horses by raising the weights and punishing the stars. That is not what racing is all about.

PETER CUNDELL, the *Sun*, **1979**.

Horses like Arkle, Lanzarote and Persian War should be made to last but, with things as they are, there are so few conditions races, and the outstanding horses simply have to be given hard races so they are killed off in two seasons.

FRED WINTER, the *Sun*, **1979**.

If I were a horse, I would rather be on bute if it meant I could go on enjoying an active life for a bit longer.

CHRISTOPHER COLLINS, **1979**.

The horse in England is not regarded as an economic animal, whereas in France it is. This was decided in the days when Sir Thomas Dugdale was Minister of Agriculture and we have been suffering from that decision ever since. It also has the disadvantage that the horse is excluded from research conducted by the Minister of Agriculture. The Jockey Club are well aware they have only themselves to blame.

RICHARD BAERLEIN, the *Guardian*, **1979**.

I'm a great believer that horses should enjoy racing. You should encourage them to want to race – hooking them up or giving them an easy run only teaches them bad habits. The greatest thing you can give a horse is morale.

DICK WHITFORD, **1980**.

A four-year study undertaken by the Levy Board has discovered that blistering and firing have no effect on the tendons of race-horses. This goes for line firing, acid firing, tendon splitting and carbon fibre implants. Does this mean that much time and money have been wasted and much pain and discomfort caused to horses, by a form of treatment that is more or less useless in that it only strengthens the skin but not the tendons?

ROGER MORTIMER, **1980**.

In the old days, with stiff upright hurdles, horses learnt to jump off their hocks and that is why the top hurdlers of that era could go on to be top chasers, a thing you rarely find today.

FRANK LATHAM, **1981**.

I wish there wasn't such a thing as the three-year-old filly. The difference between them – and it doesn't matter if they're top or bottom class – and the good old reliable gelding is vast, unbridge-able. You know where you are with the colts and geldings, but fillies' form rarely works out.

MAJOR DAVID SWANNELL, doyen of handicappers.

Most French vets would consider that it is their duty to maintain a horse at a peak of fitness with the aid of all modern medical techniques.

DESMOND STONEHAM, racing correspondent, **1982**.

The only thing that makes a horse expensive is pedigree. But there is no such thing as a bad pedigree. Some families are better than others because they have had more chance.

JACK DOYLE.

You like them when you buy them, then they go plain on you,

like kids, and you think God what did I see in that one, but usually they come nice again.

GILLIAN KELLEWAY, trainer's wife, **1983**.

You get pulled about every day of your life by immature horses – by the time they've learnt what it's all about ninety per cent have gone to stud. It's not an old man's job.

DON CURTIS, blacksmith, **1983**.

If I believed in reincarnation I would like to come back as a racehorse – the best food, the best accommodation, all for one hour's work a day and a race once a month. It would be hard to beat.

RAY HUTCHINSON, amateur jockey and veterinarian.

Horses are ridiculous in themselves. Only the genius of Stubbs could make them look elegant. Delacroix painted them as the prancing partners of martial triumph. Horses are intrinsically funny looking.

ROY HATTERSLEY MP, the *Guardian*.

Twelve bad horses can make a bloody good race.

DAVID MCHARG, Scottish clerk of the course.

Horses who die racing usually feel no pain.

IVOR HERBERT, the *Mail on Sunday*.

I treat them all the same and love my horses for different reasons, not necessarily for their ability. When I lose one, it's like losing one of the family. They're more generous than humans, they give everything.

JENNY PITMAN, *News of the World*.

Sprinters are more consistent partly because they're often older horses and partly because in most sprints you're going dead straight. A lot more can happen in longer races.

GEOFFREY GIBBS, handicapper, **1985**.

Many horses are fast but they don't all win races.

ANTHONY WEBBER, ex-jockey, **1986**.

Intelligence has nothing to do with speed. Some very slow horses are intelligent, some good ones aren't.

LESTER PIGGOTT in *Lester: The Official Biography*.

At least sixty per cent of horses don't really want to do their best. Winning doesn't mean all that much to them.

LESTER PIGGOTT.

They are not what they were. They used to be like wild things, climbing up the walls of their boxes. The lads used to be shaking in the corners, terrified of them. They were like tigers. They had fire in their bellies in those days.

RYAN PRICE, **1986**.

On the Turf there is only one rightful king – the racehorse; and if he is not served in the manner due to him, neither he nor his kingdom will prosper.

JOHN HISLOP, *The Times*, **1987**.

O Father of all, thank you for the dumb creatures which Thou givest us, and which are the friends of man. Give to us the understanding which may preserve us from causing them needless pain.

Prayer said over LORD LONSDALE's grave.

Affirmed

I've never ridden any horse that compares with Affirmed. He was a truly great champion.

STEVE CAUTHEN, **1985**.

Alleged

I bought Alleged as a yearling for $40,000 at Keeneland after he'd gone through the ring for $34,000. When he got home he looked awful; he came off the van like a drowned rat. I wondered why I'd ever liked him!

MONTY ROBERTS, consigner of Alleged as a two-year-old, **1977**.

Allez France

Ah, that lady. She have the speed I never see in another horse. She come from two mile, come from a mile or one and a half mile – the moment the machine start to run the speed is the same. Fantastic! I think if you run her in top five furlong race, she murder them. She so fit, so full of boom boom.

ANGEL PENNA on Allez France, **1975**.

I take Mr Wildenstein's horses in December 1973 and he tell me, 'Allez France win the Arc next year.' It no easy. I have obligation to win. You keep a filly eleven months and train her every day for 6 October. Is tough. So I never think about Arc until ten days before. And everything OK in the end.

ANGEL PENNA.

Allez France was not only very plain with large floppy ears which would not stand up, she was also a complete nuisance. She came crashing out of the stall and nearly went crazy when she discovered her sheep was missing. Allez France either had her head up in the air, or on the ground looking for the sheep. She was aesthetically unattractive, but she merely made up for it on the track.

RICHARD STONE REEVES, painter, **1977**.

I think we received more offers of portraits of Allez France than Madame Pompadour had of herself, and Madame Pompadour was never on television. Allez France was.

DANIEL WILDENSTEIN, **1977**.

Alverton

Alverton was killed at the height of his career. It's better than being killed when you only look like doing it. He'd done it.

PETER EASTERBY, who trained the 1979 Gold Cup winner.

Alverton was a typical jumping type – a longish horse, with plenty of bone, a pronounced jumping bump and most important of all, full of guts. I suppose you could describe him as a tough, plain horse.

PETER EASTERBY, 1982.

Alydar

The relationship between Alydar and me was unbelievable. I used to hide myself behind a tree and call him. I make him crazy, bucking and kicking inside his stall looking for me.

JORGE VELASQUEZ, jockey, 1981.

Ardross

He made up the ground under the rhythmic application of Lester's whip and almost pulled back the last half-length as Piggott laid on four strokes, rapid fire.

ROBERT CARTER on Ardross's second place finish in the 1982 Prix de l'Arc de Triomphe.

Arkle

He's a bit of a swank. He would always play to the crowd. But I couldn't think he'd ever fall.

TOM DREAPER on Arkle, 1975.

Pat Taafe never agreed with me. He thought Arkle was such a brilliant jumper and so clever that he'd always get himself out of trouble. He was probably right, but I have no regrets. I was not prepared to risk my best friend.

ANNE, DUCHESS OF WESTMINSTER, on not running her horse Arkle in the **1965** Grand National.

Bula

He was big, ugly and fat. More like a warhorse than a racehorse.

BULA described by his lad Vince Brooks on his first arrival in the yard, **1985**.

Dahlia

I know Dahlia never beat Allez France on the track, but she would have beaten her easily for looks.

RICHARD STONE REEVES, painter, **1977**.

Dawn Run

Perhaps the unremitting flow of human tragedy that comes from the pages of our newspapers and from our television screens has hardened the heart against the death of a horse, however great.

But I still felt a fierce sorrow on behalf of the Mullins because if there is a finer or more admirable family in racing then I have never met them nor heard about them.

ALASTAIR DOWN, on the death of Dawn Run, *The Sporting Life*.

Devon Loch

Among the horses he almost bought but turned down because of a sixth sense was Devon Loch: There was something about his action I didn't like. Maybe he was a bit lame at the time. I don't know. But there was something wrong all right. I thought he would be a horse that would break down a lot.

TOM DREAPER, in *My Life and Arkle's*.

Eclipse

It will be Eclipse first, the rest nowhere.

DENNIS O'KELLY, owner of Eclipse.

Golden Fleece

After Pat Eddery had given Golden Fleece a three furlong spin on the course early on the morning of the race, he came back to report that he had coughed three times. After consulting our vet, Bob Griffin, on the phone in Ireland, we decided to take a chance and run him, thinking it might have been the very warm weather that had caused some dryness in his throat. As it turned out, it is certain that he did have a virus when he ran, and that was why he took so long to get over it.

VINCENT O'BRIEN on how Golden Fleece won the **1982** Derby.

Gyr

The hardest horse I rode was undoubtedly Gyr in the Derby, where we were second to Nijinsky and in the Grand Prix de St-Cloud which I won on the same horse. He was not just wrong in the head but in his mouth. Even when you got off you never stopped riding. By the time you had cantered down to the gate, you'd had enough. The real worry was that so much was expected of him and you didn't have to do much wrong to undo him. I've never been so tired as when I came home after winning the Grand Prix de St-Cloud. It was like riding two horses!

BILL 'WEARY WILLIE' WILLIAMSON, **1974**.

John Henry

John Henry was no prize. He was back at the knee, ungainly in appearance and had a disposition to rival Dennis the Menace.

MEL SNOWDEN on the world's highest earning horse, **1982**.

Kelso

Once upon a time there was a horse named Kelso . . . but only once.

JOE HIRSCH, American journalist, quoted by Juliette Harrison in *Pacemaker*, **1984**.

Known Fact

I once worked Known Fact over four furlongs with Sharpo and he murdered Sharpo. I think it's true that any top class Classic horse should be able to go with a sprinter.

JEREMY TREE, **1985**.

Levmoss

There is a school of thought that says that Bill Williamson 'stole' the race by impersonating a jockey in trouble for about a furlong before he really kicked on.

PAUL HAIGH on Levmoss's defeat of Park Top in the **1969** Prix de l'Arc de Triomphe.

Lyphard

The fact of the matter was that Lyphard was a rig [a colt who has only one testicle]. He was the gamest horse I've ever trained but at times this used to affect him. When it gets badly placed it can hurt a horse, and I'm sure that's what happened at Tattenham Corner when he went out all of a sudden.

ALEC HEAD, **1975**.

Mandarin

I didn't know what to do when the bit broke. I couldn't pull him up, and I was too windy to throw myself off.

FRED WINTER on Mandarin's win in the French Grand National.

The greatest horse I ever trained. The greatest character – full of guts.

FULKE WALWYN on Mandarin.

Milk Heart

Stalliony? You could take him to the Playboy in a pair of blinkers and he wouldn't bother to take them off.

GEOFF LEWIS, refuting a suggestion that Milk Heart is stalliony, *Daily Express*, **1984**.

Mill House

The best performance I ever saw was when the 'Duke' [David Nicholson] rode him to win the Whitbread at Sandown in 1967. I never saw a jumping display like that in my life – Arkle included.

JACK DOYLE on Mill House, **1981**.

Mill Reef

We soon realized that either Mill Reef was pretty good or the other two-year-olds were useless. As it turned out both were right. He was outstanding and the others were absolutely useless.

IAN BALDING, **1982**.

He was the greatest all-round racehorse I have ever seen.

MICHAEL OSWALD, manager of the Royal Studs on Mill Reef, **1986**.

The Minstrel

In training he used to sweat freely, giving the impression that he lacked courage. Yet he was as tough and game as they come.

VINCENT O'BRIEN, **1985**.

Monksfield

This horse is part of the family, like a son to us. We would not ask him to do anything that would not be in his best interests. He's a joy to be with. On the worst days he puts us in a good humour.

DES MCDONOGH, trainer, on Monksfield, **1979**.

Mrs McArdy

I clapped eyes on this yearling and her beauty and conformation made me gasp.

MICK EASTERBY on his 1000 Guineas winner Mrs McArdy, **1987**.

Mummy's Pet

Mummy's Pet had the worst pair of hind legs of any horse I've ever bought. But he walked round the parade ring at Newmarket in about ten strides. And look what he's turned out to be – he's like a winner-producing factory.

JACK DOYLE, **1982**.

Nearula

Nearula should have won the Derby. It was the press who stopped him. While he was being plated before the race, some photographers whom I had allowed into the yard, asked the blacksmith to pose. He looked up and pricked Nearula. You can't win the Derby with a lame horse.

CAPTAIN CHARLES ELSEY, **1981**.

Nijinsky

Nijinsky will leave an indelible mark on my life because he was a hell of a character, very difficult to train and a bloody magnificent horse.

MICHAEL KAUNTZE, recalling his time as assistant trainer to Vincent O'Brien, **1974**.

For a terrifying moment on the way to the start at Epsom, it looked as if Nijinsky might be in trouble as he set his head resolutely for the stables. Typically, however, even this move had been anticipated by Vincent, so that three of his stablemen were in the right place just at the right time to seize the colt and lead him back down the path to the starting-gate.

TIM FITZGEORGE-PARKER, **1975**.

Nijinsky was a brilliant racehorse, of course, but he was highly strung. He never really talked to you. He always seemed to be looking at birds.

LESTER PIGGOTT, **1975**.

Nijinsky was not a classic beauty. He was a bit too high behind for that, and his eye was not the biggest you've ever seen, but you could always pick him out. With that arched neck he was full of quality. A clear and obvious champion.

RICHARD STONE REEVES, painter, **1977**.

Nijinsky was a free sweater and impetuous to get on with his work. Lester Piggott said that he was like this before a race but once he had jumped out of the stalls he immediately relaxed.

VINCENT O'BRIEN, **1985**.

Northern Dancer

He was a wilful little son of a gun. He wasn't mean or anything but he'd do tricks. You'd start to breeze him and he'd start to bolt.

JOE THOMAS, stud manager, on Northern Dancer as a racehorse, **1982**.

O. I. Oyston

This one's a cute beggar. He should work for the *Timeform* organization because he's forgotten more about racing than Phil Bull ever knew.

JACK BERRY, on his multiple winner O. I. Oyston, **1983**.

Orby

'Thank God and you sir,' an old woman said to his trainer on his return in triumph from Epsom, 'that we have lived to see a Catholic horse win the Derby.'

After Orby had won the Derby in **1907**.

Pebbles

As a foal her cheeky face always caught your eye in the paddock.

CLIVE BRITTAIN on Pebbles, **1986**.

Pendil

Pendil was standing off his fences further and further, soaring over them like a gazelle and making seasoned jumpers look silly. He was a natural and always had confidence.

VINCE BROOKS, stable lad, **1985**.

Red Rum

He survived because he possesses, in my experience, more toughness, more resilience, more downright, upright soaring courage than any horse I've ever been honoured to know. And he could be said, at this point in our island's history, to be an example to us all.

IVOR HERBERT, in *Red Rum*.

He had been subjected to sufficient pain from whip and bone disease to make him, had he been human, turn crook or layabout.

IVOR HERBERT.

I know he doesn't like it. He knows he doesn't like it. And he knows that I know he doesn't like it.

RON BARRY on Red Rum's jumping at Haydock Park, **1978**.

There are times when we take him down to the beach, especially
in winter, when he looks at you, puts his ears back, and you can
hear him thinking, 'Jesus, not again.'

GINGER MCCAIN on Red Rum, 1978.

Reference Point

You know that big horse of yours. I think he's very good – but
he's lazy and difficult to motivate.

HENRY CECIL to owner/breeder Louis Freedman on Reference Point in 1986.

Reform

Last year Reform was Europe's leading sire, yet when John Hislop
and I valued the yearlings, we couldn't put him in at more than
£500. He was so tiny.

SIR GORDON RICHARDS, 1974.

Rheingold

When I got there I turned his eye inside out. There were black
lines in it where there should have been pink. He'd got clots of
blood in his veins which weren't working, and his spleen wasn't
cleaning.

I made up some of my powder for him and gave them to the
girl in Barry Hill's office, who made sure one was put in his feed
every day.

After sixteen days I went to see him again. It was like a miracle.
He was a different horse. His eyes were bright and he looked
glorious.

I turned to Barry and said, 'Good God, I can make him find a
stone on anything he's ever done.'

His blood was like crystal and his spleen was working like a
beautifully fine sieve. The last gallop he did was unbelievable – it
was like an express train.

SYD MERCER on Rheingold before his win in the 1973 Arc de Triomphe.

Roberto

I wouldn't know how to explain the brilliance of his performance at York, but to rate him as though it never happened, as *Timeform* did, suggests that perhaps they gave credence to Mrs Hislop's ungenerous remark that he might have been stung by a bee at the start.

TONY MORRIS on Roberto's defeat of Brigadier Gerard in August 1972, *The Racing Post*, **1988**.

Rosyth

Rosyth was the oddest horse I ever had. He was useless during the winter. But as soon as the spring started to come, he became a real racehorse. I told them the explanation was that he was a spring horse, but they didn't believe me. Still, my conscience was clear . . . I really thought they had it in for me during that time, but again my conscience is clear.

RYAN PRICE, on the winner of the 1963 and 1964 Schweppes Gold Trophy, The *Weekender*, **1984**.

Sea Bird

To have been in the presence of greatness is one of the most comforting and inspiring feelings I know.

TONY MORRIS on Sea Bird's victory in the Arc de Triomphe.

Secretariat

I never experienced real immortality until I met Secretariat.

RICHARD STONE REEVES, painter.

My God! Look at that. He looks as if he could jump over a barn.

RICHARD STONE REEVES, on Secretariat, **1977**.

Sir Ken

Sir Ken was a terrific jumper. Fantastic! He stood off so far at his hurdles that you could feel your tummy going.

TIM MOLONY on three time Champion Hurdle winner Sir Ken, 1979.

Stalbridge Colonist

I worked out my plan. My horse was always going really well and we gradually made up ground. I jumped the second last four lengths behind Pat [Taafe] and deliberately waited for him to look round. Sure enough he did. As soon as he'd had his look, seen no danger and turned back, then I went.

STAN MELLOR on how he beat the great Arkle on Stalbridge Colonist in the 1966 Hennessy Cognac Gold Cup.

Tolomeo

Mine's a hell of a horse. The pot was big so why not have a shot.

LUCA CUMANI explaining why he took Tolomeo to win the Arlington Million in Chicago, 1983.

Vaguely Noble

When I galloped Vaguely Noble at Chantilly before the Arc, it was one of the most exciting experiences of my life. When they gallop a horse out there they really gallop them like the old-fashioned English trainers. The lead horse was a really good animal who was only just beaten by Classic milers the following year and went on to win top-class stakes races in the United States. We worked over one mile three furlongs and Vaguely Noble was giving weight and start to this horse and his other stable-mate, yet I went by them as though they were standing still and beat them out of sight. When I came back I told Etienne Pollet, 'This must win – *will* win the Arc.' I have never known anything like it. I had no doubt at all.

BILL 'WEARY WILLIE' WILLIAMSON, 1974.

9
Breeders

You may put all the brains you have into racing but you will be nowhere unless you have luck.

'LUCKY' LODER, owner-breeder of Pretty Polly.

> The lower classes are such fools
> They waste their money on the pools.
> I bet, of course, but that's misleading.
> One must encourage bloodstock breeding.

BERNARD FERGUSSON.

I would never enter a filly of mine for the Oaks that I intended to keep for myself or my stud.

RICHARD BAERLEIN, the *Observer*.

To suggest that that magnificent stayer of my youth, Brown Jack, bought as a yearling for 110 guineas, was bred well enough for the long-distance Classic races because he was in-bred to St Simon in the fourth generation with a third cross of St Simon's sire Galopin close up in his pedigree, is just a joke.

PHIL BULL, *Books & Bookmen*.

The first precept the owner-breeder, or for that matter the commercial breeder, must grasp is that breeding to race bears almost no relation to producing yearlings to sell.

JOHN HISLOP, *British Racehorse*.

There is practically nothing on breeding in print worth reading. The few books on the subject have as much relation to the realities of the matter as astrology has to astronomy – tap roots, inbreeding, outcrossing, sires lines, prepotency, etc., overlaid with a dressing of genetics, mostly misunderstood – it is a world of fantasy.

PHIL BULL, **1975**.

The fascination for the breeder is in thoroughbreds or game chickens because you're breeding for the intangible, evanescent qualities that exist in an animal – courage and gameness. You're not breeding for type, you're breeding for very intangible and very illusive qualities.

JOHN GAINES, owner of Gainesway Farms, **1975**.

Value is the important thing, price is the unimportant thing.

JOHN GAINES.

I have a very simple theory about conformation. It appears simplistic on the surface, but actually it is just simple. A horse is bred to go to the race track. If he goes on the race track and proves to be a major stake winner, then that tells only one thing – his conformation is correct. That is, the conformation you can't see, the conformation genotype. He has the right angles and right locomotive efforts that work *for him*. I don't care if he's a midget or a giant, his internal parts are harmonious.

JOHN GAINES.

My father was a great friend of Fred Darling, and I used to visit him once a month. He always used to say the only way to breed Classic winners was to have a few mares on a lot of grass.

RYAN PRICE, *The Sporting Life*.

This business of tracing back tail-female lines to the n-th generation, as though it told you something material about the horse himself, is a typical example of the 'blood line' buggaboo in the traditional breeding mystiques that I condemn. No geneticist could think in this way.

PHIL BULL, letter to *The Sporting Life*, **1976**.

There is only one effective way to encourage the breeding of staying horses and the racing of them at the distances over which they are most effective and that is to promote a sufficient number of races over distances long enough to reward stamina.

Timeform's Racehorses of 1976 in the comment on Sagaro.

My father has always been interested in obtaining strong male lines.

BROWNELL COMBS, son of Leslie Combs, founder of Spendthrift Farms, **1977**.

Johnny Hislop, a very able writer and a great friend of mine, will write a horse up, saying what a brilliant pedigree the animal has. I guarantee that I could write up thirty horses bred exactly the same way that are absolutely useless and who can't go as fast as me.

CAPTAIN TIM ROGERS, **1977**.

Artificial insemination has to come and will arrive sooner than many think.

BILL MCCREERY, **1978**.

Artificial insemination is a crazy idea. Who wants a hundred Mill Reefs anyway?

RICHARD BAERLEIN, the *Observer*, **1978**.

I first heard about his savagery a year or so ago when I moved into the district. Of course, I was immediately fascinated in much the same way as a child might be by the idea or story of a monster.

JEFFREY BERNARD on the stallion Supreme Sovereign, **1979**.

No white at all. That pleases the Queen so much.

MICHAEL OSWALD, The Queen's stud manager, on Bustino, **1979**.

Troy has done racing no good in the long run. Syndicated shares at £180,000 each putting a value on him of £7,200,000. It is just not right.

HENRY CECIL, quoted by John Trickett in the *Sun*, 1979.

Tesio says that jumping is not bred in horses. I do not agree.

JOHN THORNE, 1981.

I often say we are in the dream business. Everyone dreams. I dream and you dream. Every man who walks in here to sign a nomination form is dreaming of Ascot or The Curragh or Cheltenham. Dreamers have always been the people who have kept the world sane. And always did and always will.

MICHAEL OSBORNE, stallion master, 1981.

When you have a run of disasters and you have the worst thing that could ever happen, like losing your best mare, you say to yourself, 'If anything else happens, I am giving the whole thing up.' And sure enough, within a week something even worse happens! But you find hidden reserves.

KIRSTEN RAUSING, breeder, 1981.

Stud men are without doubt the unsung heroes of racing. A manager is only as good as his stud groom.

TOTE CHERRY-DOWNES, bloodstock agent, 1982.

You only have a Mrs Penny once in a lifetime – and you want to sniff at that rose every opportunity you can get.

MARSHALL JENNEY, breeder, 1982.

Now ladies and gentlemen, I will have to ask you to mind your manners, because you are right now in the presence of *roy . . . al . . . tee.*
  This here horse is not an ordinary horse, this here horse is a *King.* And just remember that back in the days when a dollar was a dollar, this here horse won a world record total of $1,288,565 and *no change.* He was also the first million dollar syndicated

stallion, $1,251,200 and *no change*. He was a champion at two, a champion and Horse of the Year at three with earnings in one season of a record $752,000 and *no change*.

That's why he's a King. And you'll not get offended if he don't pay you no never mind, because that's the way Kings are. They just don't talk to anyone they don't know. Not unless they are with one of their real good friends. Such as me.

CLEM BROOKS, stallion man, on his charge Nashua, addressing visitors to Spendthrift Farm in Kentucky, **1982**.

Racing is a show-biz thing.

BOB MCCREERY, breeder, **1982**.

Selling yearlings is a nerve-wracking business.

BOB MCCREERY.

Old Clem was really funny with Nashua. I've seen him march across the breeding shed to Nashua and give him a hard slap on the backside, shouting, 'Come on now, get on with it . . . I ain't here to waste my time while you're just in*dulgin*' yourself.'

PATRICK ROBINSON on Nashua's stallion man Clem Brooks, **1982**.

The racehorse breeding industry has never had a Kenneth Tynan to go on television and use the explicit four-letter word for sexual intercourse. The result is that horse-breeding terms, which have suddenly been forced on the layman's attention through the Shergar kidnapping, have a bewildering esoteric flavour reminiscent of a Victorian lady novelist.

DENNIS BARKER, the *Guardian*.

The Phalaris line is absolutely predominate.

JIM JOEL, **1984**.

I allow her to go to the stud for the one very good reason, I didn't want to sell her. Otherwise somebody else will have the blood, the pure blood of Allez France and, I? I would have nothing.

DANIEL WILDENSTEIN, **1984**.

There's a poster up by the stallion boxes which reads, 'Have you hugged your horse today?' That says everything as far as we're concerned.

JOHN CLARKE, manager of the Irish National Stud, **1984**.

They're all easy to ride. None that I've ridden have been difficult. They settle really well. They've got so much speed, and yet they seem to stay as well. More stay than don't – anyway, up to 1¼ miles.

PAT EDDERY on the progeny of Northern Dancer, **1985**.

It seemed like everyone heard he was small and went out to find the biggest mare they could. We just used to shake our heads in disbelief as all these giants came in.

BEN MILLER, manager of Windfield's stallion division on Northern Dancer, **1985**.

I don't know any other sire who consistently gets sons who outbreed themselves – that is, make even better sires than they were racehorses.

JOHN MAGNIER, on Northern Dancer, **1985**.

Northern Dancer must be regarded as one of the greatest, if not the greatest, sires of all time. It is incredible that such a small horse should have achieved so much success and carved such a niche for himself in the history of the thoroughbred. Apart from the ability, soundness and gameness he has passed on, he has also succeeded in stamping his stock to a truly remarkable degree. This is so rarely true of sires whose stock get a distance of ground. They are apt to come in different shapes and sizes.

VINCENT O'BRIEN, **1985**.

So why is Snaafi Dancer going to stud? It may be good for the Maktoums, it may save some face for their advisers. But it certainly isn't good for racing. If it became an established practice, it would make a nonsense of the whole game.

The *Life* speaks out against it. If the trend continues, racing could be grateful for our independent voice.

'Saturday Opinion', on the unraced colt who fetched $10.2m as a yearling, in *The Sporting Life*, **1986**.

I can get a much higher percentage of horses in foal in Ireland than anywhere else.

ROBERT SANGSTER, *Wall Street Journal*, **1986**.

I questioned the necessity of a National Stud at all. I thought (and still do) that the funds available would be better spent on standing stallions of various calibres at privately owned studs around the country.

CHRIS WATKINS, **1986**.

Without a National Stud, there is no focus and no responsibility.

DAVID GIBSON, director of the Thoroughbred Breeders' Association, **1986**.

There should be a licence system to stop indiscriminate breeding.

PRINCESS ROYAL, **1986**.

Most of us are in this business for profit and many of us feel some anxiety about the future.

LORD PORCHESTER, president of the Thoroughbred Breeders' Association, **1987**.

We are in a funny situation. It's entirely due to the Arabs that Britain now has the best racing in the world. One thousand of the best bred yearlings in the States come over here annually.

CHRIS HARPER, *The Field*, **1987**.

MONTY COURT: Have you any particular ambition in the long term – to breed horses for instance?
PRINCESS ROYAL: Oh, no. A mug's game.

The Sporting Life, **1987**.

10
Jockey Club

The same man who crusaded against the tricks and villainies of others did not scruple to do things quite as bad as the worst misdeeds which he so vigorously and unrelentingly attacked.

CHARLES GREVILLE on the unscrupulous Lord George Bentinck.

In regard to the Jockey Club, if it proceeds in the course in which it has of late been proceeding, the sooner for the sake of the Turf it is abolished, the better. There is no good in such an assembly, in fact it is an absolute nuisance. This is the third time that Rous, by deciding matters in his own favour in which he had a pecuniary claim, has raised a general war. . . . His vicious example, instead of being avoided, has been imitated – where then do you gather your hope that by submitting to these proceedings of the Jockey Club you will obtain any reform in their general conduct?

LORD GEORGE BENTINCK, **1844**.

You've got hold of entirely the wrong end of the stick. Do you seriously imagine that I'm going to tell Jeremy (he referred to one of our wealthiest private-income trainers) what he ought to charge? It would be damned impertinence. Just as if he were to tell me what I ought to pay my butler!

SIR RANDLE FEILDEN in *The Spoilsports*.

To become a member of the Jockey Club you've got to be a relation of God, and a close one at that.

From *The Wit of the Turf*.

The Duke held the *Morning Star* as if it were a week-old fish.

Time magazine reporting that the Duke of Norfolk purchased a copy of the communist paper during the 1955 newspaper strike.

The stewards will continue to resist the demand for overnight publication of the draw, as they are convinced that this can only result in more alleged non-triers, and in many cases owners and trainers would happily pay a fine and withdraw in lieu of expensive travel arrangements if badly drawn . . . furthermore, this [the published draw] would be most valuable additional information for the dopers, as it would reduce their field of operations considerably.

TOM BLACKWELL, 1966.

It would seem a good idea for the public to watch the Oaks.

SIR RANDLE FEILDEN, 1967.

The Jockey Club is fair game for a lot of people. The Jockey Club has stood the test of time and will go on standing the test of time for one reason only and that is that it acts with complete integrity in anything it does. Now a lot of people suggested broadening the base of various things in this world and those in many cases who've broadened their base have tended to lose integrity and that I think in racing would be fatal.

SIR RANDLE FEILDEN.

It has taken eighteen years to have an overnight draw. It took fifteen years of pressure for a photo-finish camera, twenty years for overnight declarations, and fifteen years for starting-stalls. Railway workers, dockers, or miners did not start 'go slow'. The Jockey Club got in first, and they subsequently patented it.

RICHARD BAERLEIN, the *Guardian*, 1967.

'Don't sell your mares.' That is sound advice, but when you see rich men with studs and members of the Jockey Club selling mares like Aunt Edith and Greengage to the Americans, where is the example?

RICHARD BAERLEIN on owner Raymond Guest's advice, the *Observer*, 1968.

I believe that the men whose lives and livelihoods they control are entitled to ask at least the same mercy criminals get – the knowledge how long their punishment is to last. Johnny Haine [National Hunt jockey] was not granted that mercy last week, and I sincerely hope that his will be the final example of a bad and useless survival.

JOHN OAKSEY, **1968**.

Comes of having all these damned jumpers about.

LORD ROSEBERY, having mislaid his binoculars at the first meeting where members of the National Hunt Committee were admitted to the Jockey Club stand at Newmarket, **1969**.

While it is clearly desirable for officials and others who contribute to the entertainment to be given a free pass, it is hardly the occasion for a free family outing. Members of the Jockey Club do a lot of hard work without a penny by way of expenses, but ought this to entitle the wife of a member and all daughters, married or single to buckshee racing for the rest of their lives?

ROGER MORTIMER, *Sunday Times*, **1969**.

Sir, I would like to suggest, at this season of good will, that the Jockey Club might well consider the admission of women members as a recognition of the great support given to racing by the club's patron, the Queen, and the Queen Mother and by other women owners. The introduction of our more gentle influence to that august body could prove the best possible reform.

DAME JOAN VICKERS, letter to *The Times*, **1969**.

Two or three of the 100-plus members of the Jockey Club would be only too pleased to see the back of Wigg. They do not like him because he can see through them and their pettiness. They are not an asset to racing in any shape or form.

RICHARD BAERLEIN, the *Guardian*, **1970**.

Perhaps at the next meeting we shall find at the entrance [to Newmarket] a close harmony group of Jockey Club members with collecting boxes, giving their arrangement of 'Buddy, can you spare a dime?'

ROGER MORTIMER, commenting on the appearance of a board on the Rowley Mile course advertising a firm of bookmakers, **1970**.

Even now pomposity too often clings to privilege. The noise made as the Club's titled stick-in-the-muds of not so long ago turn in their graves, is still sometimes allowed to drown the calls for progress.

JOHN PURVIS, **1970**.

With some justification the Jockey Club has been described as 'the purest example of the eighteenth century to survive in Britain.'

JOHN PURVIS.

Our inquiries are not like courts of law, they're more like court martials.

LORD CADOGAN, on the Jockey Club's judicial system, *Sheffield Morning Telegraph*, **1971**.

French racing has much more to offer financially than its English counterpart; but to patronize it to the extent of damaging the sport in this country by sending good horses to be trained in France, or to race them there exclusively, displays a lack of patriotism. . . . As regards the matter of supporting racing in England, it seems not inappropriate to suggest that, for a start, members of the Jockey Club might set an example by having their horses – at least the best of them – trained in this country.

JOHN HISLOP, *The British Racehorse*, **1971**.

There is always a time, or to be more precise in this case, a price at which principles simply have to be shelved or rules bent because we are living in an era when each and every racecourse has no option but to bend over backwards to satisfy a potential sponsor.

SIR RANDLE FEILDEN, **1972**.

It has been suggested to me that the Jockey Club was not sufficiently interested in their welfare. That, I hope, is not fair comment, but what is fair comment without a shadow of doubt is that Jim Harris and his generation of Jockey Club B licencemen have sometimes had a pretty raw deal from racing, and in return for long service some form of insurance should surely be thought out to protect them against illness and old age.

BILL CURLING, **1973**.

We were made to feel like criminals in London. We sat there all day without even being offered a cup of tea.

JOSH GIFFORD recalling the Hill House trial, **1974**.

The Jockey Club has always represented the Jockey Club and no one else.

RICHARD BAERLEIN, **1974**.

Perhaps the Jockey Club members possess a death wish and in their hearts wish for the sport to be nationalized and to be controlled by earnest civil servants commuting to Portman Square from Croydon and Rickmansworth.

ROGER MORTIMER, **1974**.

I don't have time to think 'God, it's time I had a haircut' or about how I dress. If I want to go to Wincanton in cap and gumboots, I go in cap and gumboots.

GAY KINDERSLEY, after resigning from the Jockey Club to become a trainer, **1974**.

When I first started trainers and jockeys used to come in shaking with fear. Now they know they are going to get a fair hearing, and it is right that they should be represented.

LORD LEVERHULME, **1974**.

The Jockey Club simply is not regarded in government circles as genuinely representative of the thousands of men and women whose livelihood depends on racing. Nor, frankly, is there much evidence that they have tried very hard to alter that state of affairs.

JOHN OAKSEY, *Sunday Telegraph*, **1974**.

The Jockey Club has never, on any issue, taken any responsibility for anything. There is no single activity on the Turf which it has put through on its own initiative.

LORD WIGG, **1974**.

The state of racing in this country? Lousy. It all boils down to money. I think it is the attitude. It is run by the wrong people.

'If you try to ride like me you will end up breaking your neck' – Lester Piggott

(*above*) 'The death-knell of racing will be labour trouble. You've got to have well-paid, contented staff. You haven't got it' – Lord Wigg. In 1975 the stable lads went on strike and disrupted racing at Newmarket, dragging Willie Carson from his mount. (*below*) 'Yes, I do love fillies . . . I've done well with them, so people send me more' – Barry Hills. Enstone Spark (left), trained by him, wins the 1000 Guineas from Fair Salinia and Seraphima in 1976

(*above*) 'As far as I was concerned there was no point in living if I couldn't be a jockey' – Bob Champion. After a miraculous recovery from cancer, Champion and Aldaniti win the 1981 Grand National. (*below*) 'I am converted to the view that Becher's Brook is an unfair obstacle which can and should be modified' – John Oaksey. A pile-up at Becher's in 1976

(*above*) 'The greatest horse I ever trained. The greatest character – full of guts' – Fulke Walwyn on Mandarin, ridden by Fred Winter pictured on the way to victory in the 1962 Cheltenham Gold Cup. (*below*) 'Foinavon has no chance. Not the boldest of jumpers, he can be safely ignored, even in a race noted for shocks' – Charles Benson. Foinavon, an outsider at 100/1, won the 1967 Grand National after virtually the rest of the field fell at the 23rd fence

The government has always let the Jockey Club run racing and let them get on with it. Undoubtedly the Jockey Club are great people and have never needed legislation to help them, but they certainly need it now.

ERIC COUSINS, trainer, hoping for more money for the industry, **1974**.

I've lost all faith in the Jockey Club now. They had their chance and they failed us.

BOB MCCREERY, on the poor state of the racing industry, **1974**.

The stewards believe that any winning owner should receive, after deductions, half the annual cost of keeping a horse in training.

LORD LEVERHULME, senior steward, speaking at the Sandown Park conference on racing, **1975**.

Naturally I am not anti-Jockey Club like some people in racing. I wouldn't be a member if I were.

CHRISTOPHER COLLINS, **1975**.

At the banquet as a young man, I sat between the Duke of Norfolk and the Archbishop of Canterbury. Ignoring my presence, they talked across me throughout the meal, calling each other 'Your Grace' all the time. Then and there I vowed I would not be addressed thus and ever since have insisted, when possible, on the use of my Christian name, Andrew.

THE DUKE OF DEVONSHIRE, **1975**.

You have been accustomed to having your own way but at some time in his life a man will meet a person who will not let him have his own way. That moment has arrived for you.

VISCOUNT TONYPANDY, as Secretary of State for Wales, in a clash with Bernard, Duke of Norfolk before the investiture of the Prince of Wales.

I think the Jockey Club do a wonderful job in running the rules of racing but I am sure that a properly representative consultative council should be set up to deal with wider problems.

CYRIL STEIN, quoted by Brough Scott in the *Sunday Times*, **1976**.

If the Jockey Club's following of fans is somewhat smaller than that of the Osmonds or the Bay City Rollers, there is little marked antipathy except from one or two leftish journalists who do not possess the knack of enlisting popular support; rather the reverse in fact. That does not mean that the Jockey Club has a long life, at least in its present form, ahead of it.

ROGER MORTIMER, *The Racehorse*, **1976**.

If you start working out the (average) age of the Jockey Club, it's absolutely horrifying.

LORD HOWARD DE WALDEN, **1977**.

Apart from Sonny Richmond-Watson and Jocelyn Hambro in a smallish way, I'm the only person who owns a Flat racehorse among the stewards. Quite a thought, isn't it?

LORD HOWARD DE WALDEN.

It has got so ingrained on people's minds that the Jockey Club is an aristocratic elite, privileged load of nonsense, that we have trouble living this image down.

LORD HOWARD DE WALDEN.

If you took a poll among punters, they would support the continuance of the Jockey Club by an enormous majority. Few of them are certain what it does. They vaguely regard it as a sort of retirement organization for eighteenth century dukes. But in general they have the impression that the vast fortunes of these gentlemen, and their lofty unawareness of real life, is likely to leave them impervious to the temptations which might beguile salaried officials.

NOEL WHITCOMB, **1977**.

He was Britain's most popular racehorse owner, yet was never elected to the Jockey Club, an institution which would have benefited from his considerable talents. That didn't worry Mr Robinson, and today must worry him even less. His memorial will be Robinson College.

MICHAEL THOMPSON-NOEL on Sir David Robinson, *Financial Times*, **1977**.

One point I find lacking in sport today is gentlemen *v.* players. It is not easy to find a team of gentlemen nowadays.

IOTH DUKE OF BEAUFORT, **1978**.

When a doctor is hauled before the BMA and accused of getting into bed with the wrong woman, every lurid detail is disclosed. Why can't the aristocrats of the Jockey Club be equally open?

JOHN JUNOR on the Jockey Club's secret hearings, *Sunday Express*, **1978**.

There seems to be a positive bias in Portman Square against racing in the North, which is inexplicable, especially as it should surely be Jockey Club policy to do everything possible to strengthen the quality of northern racing.

TOM NICKALLS, **1978**.

The Jockey Club is very autocratic of course – it was about five years before anyone said good morning to me.

ALEC MARSH, senior starter, **1978**.

Since World War II, there have been certain senior stewards of the Jockey Club who did not take that office very seriously. One or two were not wholly reminiscent of the commanding officer of a former cavalry regiment, converted to armour, who in 1939 insisted that the officers wore spurs in armoured cars. Not for nothing was he known as 'Beau Geste' or 'the bloody joke'. Matters are rather different today.

ROGER MORTIMER, *The Racehorse*, **1979**.

What do I do? You might just as well ask a hottentot who his tailor is.

LORD SEFTON, owner of Aintree racecourse.

The Jockey Club has no axe to grind.

CAPTAIN JOHN MACDONALD-BUCHANAN, **1979**.

The Jockey Club still insist that housed in the depths of Portman

Square they have a Race Planning Committee. I suspect that it consists of an empty room with a table and a couple of chairs. I doubt whether it is ever occupied. If it is it can only be by people who have nothing at all between the ears.

WALTER GLYNN, *The Racehorse*, **1979**.

The Jockey Club think you're quite suitable. They just think it's a bit odd you don't wear a hat.

Response to owner GEORGE CAMBANIS's application for membership of Newmarket in 1949, related by Julian Wilson in *Pacemaker*, **1979**.

The Jockey Club have got their priorities wrong. Their number one priority is the future of the Jockey Club. Their number two priority is the future of racing.

RICHARD BAERLEIN, **1979**.

I'm certain better justice comes out of the Jockey Club than from the courts of the country.

DICK WHITFORD, **1980**.

If somebody wanted to pay me for the work I do as senior steward, I wouldn't object.

CAPTAIN JOHN MACDONALD-BUCHANAN, **1980**.

As far as we are concerned, the owner, trainer, jockey and horse are a team. If one member of the team infringes the rules, then all should suffer. No owner should benefit from his jockey breaking the rules.

JOHN MACDONALD-BUCHANAN.

There is a case that it is better to be inexpertly judged than corruptly judged, but they seem to work it that you should be judged by those who have no brains and no interest.

DAVID GIBSON, breeder, on the Jockey Club, **1980**.

On the day before his final stroke I was with him at a meeting of the Injured Jockeys Fund, and the real concern and understanding

that he showed that day for several sad cases is a memory that
will never fade.

BROUGH SCOTT on Edward Courage, owner/breeder and member of the Jockey
Club, **1982**.

The Jockey Club promised to meet my expenses. Then they had
the gall to send a cheque for £500. I told them to keep it . . . sent
it to the Injured Jockey's Fund.

RYAN PRICE on the Hill House affair, *Sunday Express*, **1982**. Price had his own
tests done on the horse.

All I know is that I've met the Jockey Club people, which in itself
would have been unheard of at one time.

JOE (now Lord) GORMLEY, **1982**.

I entirely disagree with what has been said about starting stalls. I
do not consider it an English method of starting a race and I never
shall.

THE LATE DUKE OF NORFOLK, **1982**.

Congratulations to the Jockey Club for electing you a member.

Telegram from PHIL BULL to the eighty-five-year-old Sir Foster Robinson, **1982**.

I like to be an entrepreneur. There's so much to do, change,
improve. I try to bring these things to work on the Jockey Club,
who are the most charming, committed, disinterested people I
know.

SIMON WEATHERBY, the late secretary to the Jockey Club, **1982**.

I think the days of the lofted perch have gone for ever. The people
at the top, in other words the Jockey Club members, are realizing
that life must be a bit more democratic than in former years.
Perhaps they have been their own worst enemies. I don't know.
One or two of them are certainly stuffed shirts but then they've
never dealt with anyone different so they probably didn't know.

JOE GORMLEY, *The Sporting Life*, **1983**.

I was to learn later that softening up Ministers with jaunts to the racecourse and plenty of agreeable claret was now high on the agenda.

JANE MCKERRON in the *Tatler* on a visit to Portman Square, **1983**.

If you want to know, I am appalled at the sponsorship [of The Derby]. What I cannot understand is how they expect to sell more batteries or whatever it is.

LORD HOWARD DE WALDEN, *Daily Express*, **1984**.

Jenny Pitman remembers going to apply for her trainer's licence at the Jockey Club, where the stewards on the other side of the polished table whispered in her presence, which in her country way she thought was rude.

DAVID MILLAR, *The Times*, **1984**.

Of course, the Duke had his gifts. But were they such as to justify wielding immense power over a subsidised branch of the entertainment industry in competition with other sectors presided over by men of high IQ who had won their offices by merit? And were they mice or men who trembled in his presence?

RICHARD BAERLEIN on the late Duke of Norfolk, **1985**.

Occasionally we have to come down and kick someone, and an umpire can't do that.

LORD MANTON, senior steward of the Jockey Club, on being asked if they had taken up the role of an umpire, **1985**.

I find it quite sad to go racing today compared with when I was a young man. Everyone knew everyone else then. Now the only people I really know are the professionals, the trainers and so on. I don't really know who my fellow owners are. It used to be more fun when you were running against your friends.

LORD HOWARD DE WALDEN, **1985**.

The North doesn't seem to be getting any active help from the Jockey Club. Quite the opposite. When they do act, it's usually to downgrade our races. It may be a rich man's sport, but that's no reason for concentrating all the wealth around Newmarket and telling everyone else to get stuffed.

BILL ELSEY.

It's important to have racing controlling its own destiny. To call in outsiders, particularly lawyers and retired judges, to sit in judgement would be a very bad thing.

MATHEW MCCLOY, solicitor, on Jockey Club justice, **1986**.

That's what the Jockey Club is interested in – the breed and discipline.

BROUGH SCOTT, **1986**.

Senior stewards have a lot of power, and when one interviews them it sometimes turns out that they have no idea what they are talking about, and by the time they have learned it is too late because their three years are up.

BROUGH SCOTT, who must have convinced the Jockey Club, as shortly afterwards they extended the term to four years, **1986**.

I suppose those of us who loyally support National Hunt racing through the long season have little effect on those who, from a lofty perch, actually control British racing's destiny.

IVOR JORDAN, assistant secretary of Fakenham Supporters Club in its year book, **1986**.

Quite a lot of the stewards smarmed round me afterwards and said they'd been on my side all along. Shame they didn't make more of an effort beforehand.

MRS FLORENCE NAGLE, who took the Jockey Club to the High Court to obtain the right of women trainers to hold licences in their own name, **1986**.

Oh no, the Jockey Club has to be self-electing otherwise you would get delegates. The media would have to have someone – someone like you in – and who wants that?

SIR JOHN 'JAKIE' ASTOR to Brough Scott, **1987**.

Oh, I think things have moved a long way. I mean my grandfather would never have dreamed of talking to someone like you.

LORD CADOGAN to Brough Scott, **1987**.

Hunting guilty men in spheres where scandal has arisen is now a popular national pastime. Yet Piggott's folly does not demand that the whole racing world be turned upside down. A most severe warning has been uttered. Let the racing fraternity heed it.

Daily Telegraph leader, **1987**.

We keep in touch closely with our grass roots. Go back to the days before the War, or between the Wars, and it (the Jockey Club) was literally run by three or four people. They would never have been seen talking to someone like yourself of the racing press. They were the scallywags, and the bookmakers were the felons, and the punter was somebody they didn't really want to consider.

LORD CHELSEA, **1987**.

There are enough Jockey Club members and others who want Sunday racing to have won the vote easily. The vote was at 8.45pm. Too many preferred to go out to dinner. For the sake of a dinner they may have prevented Sunday racing.

LORD WYATT, **1987**.

The Jockey Club members with horses in the Henry Cecil stable are in a very tricky position unless the whole matter is swept under the carpet.

   If you were a member of the Jockey Club, had horses in Henry Cecil's stable and received that famous letter asking you to contribute extra presents over and above those registered at Weatherbys, what would you do, knowing you were being asked to break the rules of racing?

RICHARD BAERLEIN, The *Weekender*, **1987**.

In view of the continuing concern about Lester Piggott's retainer arrangements with Mr Cecil, the stewards have also considered the position of all other owners who had horses in training with

Henry Cecil at the time, specifically in connection with Rules 201(vi), 220(i) and 220(iii). Leading Counsel's opinion has been obtained and the Jockey Club has been advised that the circumstances do not give rise to any breaches of the Rules of Racing on their part.

Jockey Club report, **1987**.

I was all for them broadening their base, but now they have done this and shown themselves ready to listen, I believe their influence should continue.

VISCOUNT WHITELAW, **1988**.

I still think the Jockey Club is the best organization to run racing. Mr du Cann said to me after the second hearing that he'd never been in a tribunal as well conducted as that one.

BARNEY CURLEY, **1988**.

Everyone seemed to believe beforehand that we had an excellent chance of winning and I was hopeful. But I got the impression after a very short time that they weren't particularly interested in changing their minds.

JOHN FELLOWS, trainer of Royal Gait, after the Jockey Club had turned down his appeal, *Sporting Life*, **1988**.

Once the Ascot stewards had adjudged Asmussen guilty of careless riding they were bound by Rule 153 which left them no alternative but to disqualify Royal Gait and suspend Asmussen. To illustrate further the serious consequences of this rule: Had the Ascot stewards deemed Asmussen and Starkey guilty of careless riding, and they might well have done, Rule 153 would have compelled them to disqualify both Royal Gait and Sadeem. The 'winner' of the 1988 Ascot Gold Cup would then have been Sergeyevich, who had been beaten 20 lengths!

REG GRIFFIN, *Sporting Life*, **1988**.

11
Stewards

Once when a jockey, riding for Lord Glanely, wanted to object, Lord Glanely replied: 'Not bloody likely. I saw enough of those buggers yesterday to last me a lifetime.'

From *Great Racing Disasters*.

There are men who have grown old, with their facilities impaired through age, who nevertheless expect as a right to be invited to officiate.

SIDNEY GALTREY on the Jockey Club in the twenties, quoted by Roger Mortimer in *Pacemaker*, **1982**.

Fellow sportsmen of Alexandria. The gentlemen in the above photograph are not only absolutely incompetent, they are also extremely dishonest.

Caption to photograph of local stewards in 1937 Egyptian newspaper, quoted by ROGER MORTIMER in *Pacemaker*, **1980**.

> If past their lunch-room you are walking
>   You'll hear the acting stewards talking
> Sir Randolph says: 'This beef-steak pud
>   Is really most uncommon good'
> Lord Crust, whose cough is getting chronic,
>   Says: 'Someone's drunk my gin-and-tonic,'
> While Major Plunge says: 'I've been told
>   To put my shirt on Rotten Gold;
> I heard his trainer, Twisty, say
>   He's going to have a go today.'
> The stewards lunch till half-past three,
>   When they commence to have their tea.

GEOFFREY GILBEY in *The Racing Man's Bedside Book*.

The form book should be written in Braille for the benefit of the stewards.

CLIVE GRAHAM.

'The stewards are of the opinion that you are both equally to blame in this reprehensible affair. As I have said, you, Ingham, have been riding long enough to know better. You, Mr Hislop, are supposed to be a gentleman.' And he looked at me as if he had no illusions about my being one.

JOHN HISLOP in *Far from a Gentleman.*

The racing world is, after all, a small one where everyone tends to know, at least by reputation, everyone else. With the best will in the world it must be impossible sometimes for stewards not to feel prejudiced against persons who come up in front of them for judgement. Perhaps appeals ought to go up before someone who understands racing but is not too closely involved in it.

ROGER MORTIMER, *Sunday Times.*

'No young chap can give time to racing today,' Sir Randle [Feilden] said. He had been on a course where they had trouble finding a local steward for the meeting. 'There was not another chap with a collar and tie on the course,' he said.

CHRISTOPHER WORMAN and JOHN WINDER, 'What's the Jockey Club?', *The Times*, **1969**.

The stewards at Salisbury were Mr 'Larch' Loyd, Lord Tryon and Lord Margadale. To suggest, as the Duke of Norfolk appeared to suggest last week, that the decision made by these men to refer the Skyway running to the Jockey Club was inspired by jealousy is, in my considered opinion, a ridiculous and insulting slur on three honourable men.

JOHN OAKSEY, **1970**.

I can't understand how they think people are going to afford to keep horses in training if they are not going to race. I never knew them [during twenty-nine years as a jockey] to abandon because of wet – either a course is under water or it is raceable. Nowadays,

plenty of meetings are abandoned when racing is perfectly possible. They are 'chicken'.

BOB TURNELL, *Daily Express*, **1974**.

No case can be made out these days for a background of Eton
and the Lancers counting for more than first-hand experience of
race-riding as a qualification for stewardship.

CHRISTOPHER POOLE, **1974**.

Racecourse stewardesses would be absolutely hopeless. Women
aren't any good at disciplining men.

MERCY RIMELL, *Sunday Express*.

Go to some point-to-points and the stewards have no practical
knowledge at all, and have never seen a rule book. Very likely
there are two neighbouring MFHS who would be very adequate
judges at a puppy show and are dedicated people – but they know
nothing about racing.

SIR GUY CUNARD, amateur jump jockey, **1974**.

I see no reason why an Army officer or a gentleman of title
necessarily has the ability to race-read and hence arbitrate on a
result that could cause considerable financial loss to owners,
jockeys and backers.

CHRISTOPHER POOLE, *Evening Standard*.

With few exceptions, stewards are recruited from local gentry,
and were once referred to as the Three Blind Mice. And although
some of them can see a little further nowadays, I wonder if they
know what they're looking at.

ROBIN GRAY, *News of the World*, **1974**.

A panel of professional stewards to replace the present outmoded
system would hold clear advantages. Consistent racing justice
would then be seen to be done. This is a vital matter in which,
for once, the Jockey Club could give an international lead rather

than waiting for the Irish Turf Club, or someone else, to act first.

CHRISTOPHER POOLE, *Evening Standard*.

This year the senior steward will give his traditional pre-race warning to the jockeys [before the Grand National]. He talks sense and tells everyone to go steadily in the early stages but no one takes a blind bit of notice. Everybody bursts out laughing as soon as he walks out.

JOHN FRANCOME, *Sunday People*, **1980**.

There is a popularly promoted illusion that if anybody is not paid he is (a) a moron and (b) dishonest.

JOHN MACDONALD-BUCHANAN, ex-senior steward, **1980**.

[The lawyers] had transformed the hearing into some appalling parody of Perry Mason.

VALENTINE LAMB on the 1981 Irish 2000 Guineas appeal, *The Irish Field*, **1981**. (Kings Lake won the race, To-Agori-Mou objected and was made the winner. At the appeal, the decision was reversed.)

Any Jockey Club member of any country who believes, after viewing the Irish 2000 patrol film, that King's Lake was entitled to keep the race should either consult a very good occulist or take a course in the proper interpretation of the Club's rules as they stand.

PETER O'SULLEVAN on the **1981** Irish 2000 Guineas appeal.

What lunacy is this? What on earth are the Irish racing authorities playing at? Only cleansing resignations and a new beginning will usher in the long process of re-instating the Irish Turf Club's shattered authority in world racing.

JOHN MCCRIRICK on the **1981** Irish 2000 Guineas appeal.

At Worcester one day after the stewards had insisted on watching the film through at least half a dozen times following a very reasonable objection I'd made to the winner, one of them turned and asked me if I had any further comments to make. I said,

'Yes, Sir, I've got two actually. The first is that I'm bored with this film and could you please put something different on and, secondly, when will the usherette be bringing in the ice-creams and popcorn?' I recall that I didn't win that objection.

JOHN FRANCOME in *Born Lucky*.

Grand National hero Dick Saunders took the unprecedented step of banning all his judges and fellow stewards from drinking on the job. 'I don't want you to turn your car boots into cocktail cabinets,' he blasted. 'It looks so unprofessional, especially in front of Princess Anne [who presented the prizes].'

Daily Mail, news item.

All stewards with little or no first-hand experience of race riding should be lined up on mounts at the new apprentice training school and let loose. When in full flight, they could experience the difficulty for themselves which, hopefully, would give them a better insight into the resultant problems.

SIR GUY CUNARD, The *Weekender*, **1983**.

Steward to prominent trainer: Will your horse be fancied in the three mile hurdle today?
    Reply: No sir, he's not off.

Conversation at North Country meeting reported by NOEL WINSTANLEY, *Pacemaker*, **1984**.

I was hauled before the stewards at Cheltenham, one of which was Colonel Thompson, and they fined me £50. A few weeks later we were racing at Newcastle and Colonel Thompson took me to one side and asked what I thought of their decision. 'I think the stewards are a load of shits,' said I. 'Fair comment,' said he, 'let's go and have a drink.'

NEVILLE CRUMP, **1985**.

Far too many stewards won't sneak on their less competent pals and as a result they'll put themselves out of business.

GENERAL SIR CECIL BLACKER, former steward, in *The Sporting Life*, **1988**.

Steward at Hamilton:

   'Now then, boy. What were our orders?'

   'Oh, "Sit and wait", sir.'

The stewards sent the boy out. They conferred, but couldn't decide. They called the boy back together with the trainer, a Mr Cartwright we'll call him.

   'Yes, now, son. You were told to sit and wait. But how long did Mr Cartwright tell you to wait?'

   'Oh, till Ayr next week, sir!'

From *Bedside Racing*.

12
Officials

We want a man, like Caesar's wife, above suspicion, of independent means, a perfect knowledge of the form and actual condition of every public horse, without having the slightest interest in any stable. If by any possibility you can find this man above price, he would throw up his office in three months, disgusted with many horse-owners, whose sole knowledge of racing is confined to running horses for stakes, and abusing the handicappers.

ADMIRAL ROUS, on the ideal handicapper.

I've got a bill for our horse being entered at Ripon and Pontefract but it never ran having died previous with a stoppage in the bools. No man pays nothink in no way to no one for a dead horse and I am put about at getting this blue paper from your London solicitor men. No true bred sportsman would have done such a trick. I'm willing to send you a ham but I pays nothink to no one in London and have sent no back answer.

Yorkshire trainer to Miles L'Anson, clerk of the course, **1906**, from *The Fast Set*.

If you could give me any flagrant examples of bad handicaping of our horses I will write to the stewards about it, as it seems to me possible that a dead set may be made against the bigger stables by the handicappers in order to give what they are pleased to call the small men a chance. If that is the case the sooner the stewards are informed that the bigger owners are not going to stand it the better.

17TH LORD DERBY writing to his trainer, George Lambton, **1918**, in *A Classic Connection*.

At a Hurst Park meeting between the wars, a chaser carrying the colours of a well-known sporting peer fell heavily and, alas, was unable to rise. The vet arrived and reluctantly decided to apply the *coup de grâce*. It was a very cold day and fairly soon after lunch. At all events, the vet missed the horse and shot a senior groundsman in the foot.

The horse, in the meantime, perturbed by the shot and even more so by the groundsman's imprecations, struggled to his feet and trotted off briskly towards the stables. He won eleven more races in the course of the next two seasons.

ROGER MORTIMER, *The Racehorse.*

I'm not interested in a job where I don't have the authority to do a lot more than an old-style clerk of the course. He was little more than a land agent, looking after his Lord's estate. But I see myself as a sort of Val Parnell.

JOHN HUGHES, clerk of the course, *Daily Mirror*, **1968**.

I'm not going to reprimand a private employee publicly. You don't take a week's wages off your butler if he drops the plates.

SIR RANDLE FEILDEN, explaining why no disciplinary action had been taken against Mr Alec Marsh for starting a field at Ascot five minutes early, *Daily Mail*, **1969**.

A handicap should never be unduly elated by a close finish or depressed by horses finishing strung out. The criterion is a good field with open betting.

MAJOR DAVID SWANNELL, quoting Geoffrey Freer, the *Guardian*.

In all too many cases asking a racecourse doctor to pronounce on a jockey's fitness to ride is like seeking chiropody from a dentist.

JOHN OAKSEY, **1972**.

The appointments of Rees and Scott [ex-jockeys] is a welcome move by the Turf authorities and helps to atone for their lack of judgement when Fred Winter retired from riding nine years ago. Winter then applied for a post as assistant starter but was turned down because, it was generally thought, the powers that be believed he might not have the necessary control over jockeys with whom he had recently been riding.

DAVID HADERT, the *Guardian*, **1973**.

Handicapping on the Flat today is an absolutely full-time job.

MAJOR DAVID SWANNELL, **1975**.

If handicappers want more money they should do two jobs.

BLACKWELL REPORT, **1975**.

A public handicapper should be a man of independent circumstances in every sense of the word, and beyond suspicion of
accepting illicit compensation for favours received; attached to no
stable, a good judge of the dispositions of owners and trainers;
he should be a spectator of every race of any importance in the
United Kingdom; and his station should be at the distance post,
where horses are pulled, not at the winning post where they are
extended; he should never make a bet and he should treat all
remarks which may be made about his handicaps with the utmost
indifference . . . such a man is not to be found.

From *Horse Racing in Britain*.

When I say that the professionals, racing's labour force, are
subsidising the industry and keeping it alive, I don't just mean
stable lads. Officials, lads, jockeys, trainers are all working for
less than they are worth. I tell you, it won't go on for ever, we'll
get fewer and fewer good people.

JEREMY HINDLEY, **1978**.

Maybe one day they will receive the financial recognition that will
enable them to do what one handler did in Ireland. He actually
owned a real horse, and one memorable day at Leopardstown last
summer, had the unique distinction of loading his horse up at one
end of the race and leading it in as winner at the other.

BROUGH SCOTT, **1978**.

How the Jockey Club handicappers are expected to do other jobs
as well as handicap, I just do not know.

DICK WHITFORD, **1980**.

The greater part of the work involved in handicapping can be done outside normal working hours which does make it possible to take on other responsibilities.

CAPTAIN MACDONALD-BUCHANAN, *The Sporting Life*, **1980**.

A Jockey Club advertisement for stipendiary stewards appeared in *The Sporting Life* the other day and ended with the amazing words: 'Experience of racing, though desirable, is not essential'. The idiot who wrote that sentence should be made to write out the rules of racing a hundred times.

JOHN OAKSEY, *Sunday Telegraph*, **1980**.

We're the dullest association in racing.

STANLEY JACKSON on the Horseracing Advisory Council, **1981**.

A Stipe's opinion is often that of the last person he speaks to and they are easily influenced.

RYAN PRICE.

I'm not an Establishment person. Which is slightly odd since I come from a very Establishment family and work for the most Establishment organization in the world.

SIMON WEATHERBY, the late secretary to the Jockey Club, **1982**.

People say 'something always comes to the aid of the handicapper'. That is absolutely untrue – if the handicapper has blundered then he can usually expect to be made to pay for it.

MAJOR DAVID SWANNELL, *Sean Graham Racing Annual*, **1982–3**.

In the old days the handicappers were men one knew. They'd put their names at the bottom of the handicap. If you didn't like Mr Smith, then you went up to Thirsk and got Mr Jones. Now it's all different and for trainers like me it's disastrous. Last year I told them they were part-timers. And proved it too – one of them asked me if I really expected him to live on the wages he was paid.

BILL WIGHTMAN, **1984**.

If there is a more demanding job in racing than that of a busy clerk of the course I don't know it, and the days when the job provided a rest cure for retired majors are long gone. Racing is an industry that has not begun to master the best and fairest ways of distributing its income and while there are plenty of dummies who do well out of it there are some highly capable people who are not rewarded in full measure for their capabilities.

ALASTAIR DOWN, The *Weekender*, **1984**.

One chap gave a very learned speech about the cost of living index. But the cost of living index didn't seem to interest the stewards at all. Another chap mentioned the fact that he had children, and a steward – I'll never forget this – said: 'One doesn't need children.' Then as we filed out this great friend of mine muttered: 'That's the last race any of them will ever win.' Odd that they should have forgotten how much power a handicapper has.

MAJOR DAVID SWANNELL recalling handicappers' request for a rise in the 'Good Old Days', *The Field*.

I simply have to grow a further layer of thick skin when trainers criticise, but I recognize that I am the last person remaining to be kicked. The owner has kicked the trainer, the trainer has kicked the jockey, all of them have kicked the cat, so there is only the handicapper left.

CAPTAIN CHRISTOPHER MORDAUNT, *Daily Express*.

Contrary to some popular belief, a handicapper sets out to give all the horses in the race a chance.

CAPTAIN CHRISTOPHER MORDAUNT, **1985**.

You still have some steward's secretaries going round shouting at jockeys as though they were ostlers.

GEOFFREY SUMMERS, ex-secretary to the Jockeys' Association, **1986**.

You've got to study something, Geoff, doesn't matter what it is. Study pornography if you like, but study something.

LORD WIGG to Levy Board employee Geoffrey Summers, **1986**.

Our shop windows, gentlemen, are not doing justice to our product.

MICHAEL SMURFIT, chairman of the Irish Racing Board, **1986**.

The facetious maxim 'You don't have to be mad to work here, but it helps' is usually found on office walls but perhaps there should be an obligatory copy adorning National Hunt weighing rooms.

JOHN KARTER, the *Independent*.

Racing's appeal to spectators should take priority over its obligations to the breeding industry.

RON FABRICIUS, Goodwood's clerk of the course, *The Field*.

Arguing about money took me more time than anything else and it was quite difficult because everything had got terribly out of step. I had to do battle with the financiers but everyone got a considerable pay rise about a year ago.

It did need looking at very badly, but it does irk me now when I am told they aren't paid enough. A senior official, going into 1988, will be on around the middle £20,000s a year and a junior steward's secretary £16,000. Add to that a company car and security of tenure and I don't think that's at all bad.

GENERAL SIR CECIL BLACKER, former steward, in *The Sporting Life*, **1988**.

13
The Old Enemy

Bookmakers initiated this memorial and subscribed to it with their known liberality. There has always been the most perfect understanding between us. Whenever in any racing case my award has been adverse to their interest, it has been accepted in a loyal spirit. It is a very extraordinary fact that when so many millions are betted every year, amidst apparent tumult and confusion, so few disputes arise. This speaks volumes for the integrity of the Ring. And no man knows better than myself their charitable acts, and the high sense of honour with which they stand to their engagements.

ADMIRAL ROUS (**1791–1877**), Jockey Club handicapper.

It has always been my practice to play up my winnings. What has broken more men on the Turf than anything else is chasing their losses and buttoning up their winnings.

ROBERT SIEVIER, owner of Sceptre.

Never lay the odds, never travel entirely sober, never hunt south of the Thames.

GEOFF HARBORD'S advice, in *Far From a Gentleman*.

People like Hills, Corals and Ladbrokes put a hell of a lot into racing: they sponsor races every day of the week. They work their betting on a percentage return. If they make their books properly, they just cannot lose, so they don't need to get horses stopped or sink to all that sort of undercover work. Take Cyril Stein of Ladbrokes – he's a genius, the same sort of calibre as Arnold Weinstock, I should think.

FRED WINTER in *Winter's Tale*.

Betting is the life-blood of the racing industry and I believe the future of horseracing and British bloodstock depends entirely on the patronage of the punters, the paying customers at the turnstiles. Whether it is a good thing or not, the majority of people go racing not because of their love of horseflesh, not because it is a Sport of Kings, but because they want to bet.

WILLIAM HILL, Gimcrack Dinner speech.

The Tote is the engine of the Devil that is driving souls to hell.

ANGLICAN BISHOP OF AUCKLAND, New Zealand, grandfather of Tim Neligan (managing director of United Racecourses).

'Ducks', the fourth Marquess of Ailesbury, the greatest spendthrift of the Edwardian era, had about 'done-in' the last of his capital which at one time provided him with an income of around £60,000 a year. After a shocking Ascot, he was hauled up before the family solicitors to discuss ways and means for paying his enormous debts which were increasing every day.

'And now, my lord,' said a stiff old solicitor, 'you have made it necessary for us to cut down oaks in Savernake Forest – oaks that have seen eight generations of your lordship's family, oaks that are part of the history of England and now must be cut down to satisfy your horde of creditors. What have you to say to this?'

'Say?' replied the marquess. 'That'll make the bloody squirrels jump, won't it now?'

ANON.

I'm glad to hear you did not scorch your fingers over the Derby. I didn't myself either, but I shall take good care how I embark on such matters again, and I can't help advising you to do the same. It isn't very satisfactory to win and highly unpleasant to lose.

Letter from Edward Lyttelton to Nathanial Curzon, when schoolboys at Eton.

Nanny Shirlaw presided over 'nursery tea' every day with dignity and unquestioned mastery of any and every situation. I was looked upon by her as the authority on the Turf, and she was not above a flutter on the Classics. One Derby Day I only recalled my duty to provide her with a tip on the morning of the race. She always used to call me 'the Lord'; so I sent her a telegram, 'My Love – the Lord'. My Love won at good odds, and a reply arrived at the House of Commons – 'Our love to the Lord'.

LORD HOME in *The Way the Wind Blows*.

Racing is in a bad way financially. This is not due to the betting tax, though, of course, the betting tax has not helped matters. Racing was suffering from the shorts long before Mr Winston Churchill taxed betting. Personally, I welcome the tax and I believe that the tax instead of killing racing, will cure it.

GEOFFREY GILBEY.

> A very smart lady named Cookie
> Said 'I like to mix gambling with nookie.
> Before every race
> I go home to my place
> And curl up with a very good bookie.'

From *The Lure of the Limerick*.

A good jockey, a good horse, a good bet; follow a stable or a jockey in form. Bet on horses that have won before, even if they are to carry a penalty; winning horses so often win again. And last, but by no means least, don't bet with a bookmaker if you see him knocking spikes in his shoes.

JACK LEACH in *Sods I Have Cut on the Turf*.

> Aubrey's up, and money's down,
> The frightened bookies quake.
> Come on, my lads, and give a cheer
> Begad, Tis Cottage Rake.

'AUBREY BRABAZON', ANON.

Some of the most influential Jockey Club members, such as the late Earl of Rosebery indeed regarded some of the bookmakers as their friends. He and others like him respected them and, in return, the bookmakers gave them a point or two over the odds, knowing full well that this would be worth their while in the long run.

In the circumstances, it is easy to see why the idea of a tote monopoly did not appeal to the Jockey Club.

From *Horse Racing, Complete Guide to the Turf.*

Suppress betting by legal enactment and the game is up; thoroughbred stock would depreciate sixty per cent and our racecourses would be ploughed up. Racing has always been and will always be a gambling speculation.

ADMIRAL ROUS.

> Alas! what boots it that my noble steed,
> Chosen so carefully, the field outran?
> I did not reckon, bookie, on your speed:
> The proper study of mankind is man.

G. ROSTREVOR HAMILTON, *On a Distant Prospect of an Absconding Bookmaker.*

The great bookmaker Charlie Hibbert returned home one night after laying £9000 to £2000 twice, among other bets, against Reid Walker's Dinnah Forget winning 'the Jubilee'. It won. His wife greeted him cheerfully with the news that she had done his room up.

'How?' he asked.

'In green,' she answered.

'Bugger green, Mrs Hibbert,' he replied.

ANON.

Gentle Jesus, bless this house. Only one-fifth the odds will be paid a place.

Notice in Irish betting shop.

I don't regard betting as gambling. Gambling on horses is distasteful. Betting is the same as politics . . . If you lose there's only one person to blame – yourself. You've made a mistake of judgement. That's why betting is so good for politicians.

GEORGE WIGG.

The average bookmaker is a business man of complete honesty –
not a 'sharp boy'. And nearly all of them are law-abiding citizens
who compare favourably, say, with company directors.

The Justice of the Peace and Local Government Review, **1967**.

I gamble on the punter rather than the horse. I don't care how
good a horse's reputation, if I think the backer is a born loser I
will stand his bet for a fortune. I never hedge. That game is for
the weak.

BILL WATERHOUSE, Australian bookmaker, *Daily Mail*, **1967**.

Be wary of all horses who twist their heads violently from side to
side, against the bit. They're likely to use more energy fighting
the jockey than racing. Avoid those which persist in walking crab-
wise, unless they are young and high-spirited. Bolters are bad
bets: and those who try not to go down to the start probably won't
hurry back.

DICK FRANCIS, *Sunday Express*, **1967**.

Midge Boneham, in his day one of the best-known touts on
Newmarket Heath, died recently. A great little character and a
pretty good judge in the bargain, 'Midge' had a favourite saying
which was 'there never should be a last race'. He was ninety-five
when he died, so he lived up to it as long as possible. Sleep well,
Midge, you gave a lot of people a lot of pleasure, as well as
finding them a lot of winners.

MASTER HERBERT, *Racing and Football Outlook*, **1968**.

The introduction [of overnight declaration of blinkers and jockeys]
would serve only to pamper the betting shop layabout.

MICHAEL PHILLIPS, *The Times*, **1968**.

I have never shared the view that the punter is the backbone of
British racing. For all those years before the betting levy was
imposed he had rather been a parasite getting pleasure and the
hope of profit from other people's hard work.

JOHN OAKSEY, *Sunday Telegraph*, **1968**.

I am not one of the people who believe that the main reason why a chap becomes a bookmaker is because he is too scared to steal and too heavy to become a jockey.

NOEL WHITCOMB, *Daily Mirror*, **1969**.

Giving a computer to the Tote would be like giving an atom bomb to a baby.

LORD WIGG, the *Sun*, **1969**.

The difficult aspect of this business is whether to let clients carry on with credit betting when they are already in deep. The funny thing is they never blame themselves – only the bookmaker for letting them go on.

VICTOR CHANDLER, bookmaker, *Daily Mail*, **1969**.

I call a gambler a person who bets what he can't afford, or throws money on a roulette wheel. Getting out of your depth – that's gambling. We go to a lot of trouble to prevent people betting recklessly and getting out of their depth. I never was a gambler, and I don't approve of gambling.

WILLIAM HILL, *Reveille*.

As I observe the leadership, and the spokesmen, of the book-makers, I think they have a death wish. My operation is partly Bookmakers' Anonymous – to stop them from committing suicide.

LORD WIGG, *Daily Mail*, **1969**.

It is an interesting thought that the first Member of Parliament to attempt to introduce a betting tax was that prince of con men, the late Mr Horatio Bottomley.

ROGER MORTIMER, *The Racehorse*.

'Would you like to see a bookmaker in the Jockey Club?' 'Defi-nitely. We have a lot to contribute towards the future of racing. The bookmaker knows more about what the public wants. He hears all their grumbles. Jockey Club members can't hear that sort of evidence in their circles.'

JOE CORAL answering Michael McDonnell, *Daily Mail*, **1970**.

I believe in very strict control of betting shops. I have had a lot of money embezzled one way or another and now I am expanding. I want very tight control. I have had to call in a security organization to do this. I am afraid nine out of ten staff would embezzle if given the chance. Perhaps I am not such a great believer in human nature.

PAT WHELAN, Liverpool bookmaker, **1970**.

I think a Tote monopoly may come because I think bookmakers as a profession are not very intelligent. Neither was the dinosaur. The dinosaur got stuffed and if they're not careful so will the bookmakers for the same reason. But we're not going to get a Tote monopoly overnight – it's just not on.

LORD WIGG, **1970**.

If ever Lord Wigg mistook us for a dinosaur, we no longer take him for a taxidermist.

THE NATIONAL ASSOCIATION OF BOOKMAKERS' publication, *Into the 70's*.

A betting shop can be a place where men go to prove themselves, to find and act with a courage their daily lives do not often ask of them.

MERRILL FERGUSON, *Evening News*.

We would rather have this [Gordon Moody's plea for banning course commentaries from betting shops] than the recent really surprising proposal of Mr Brian Jenks that television bringing special programmes from the racecourse be installed in betting shops. Who would benefit from these programmes, Mr Jenks? As far as we can see, it could only be the layabouts.

'Roundabout', *The Racehorse*, **1971**.

The real fortunes in racing are made by flat-footed bookies who seldom have to face high hurdles and by the really rich owners.

EDDIE HARTY, the *Sun*.

I am convinced that within five years there will be a Tote monopoly in this country.

JOHN BANKS, **1972**.

When I called to see her on the Saturday before she died her mind was quite clear. I was going to Sandown and she wanted a bet. She scanned the newspaper, saw that Duggie Smith was riding Final Score and handed me a note which read: '2s 6d. each way Final Score.' The horse won at 100 to 8 and I took the winnings round to her that evening. It was her last bet and it was a winner!

GEORGE WIGG on the death of his mother.

After a big win, a punter in Co. Durham handed out money to people he met in the streets. And five of them promptly reported him to the police.

'Opinion', *News of the World*.

To succeed pre-eminently in English public life it is necessary to conform either to the popular image of a bookie or of a clergyman; Churchill being a perfect example of the former, Halifax of the latter.

MALCOLM MUGGERIDGE, **1973**.

Bookmaking is not gambling. You give the public the odds they expect.

NICHOLAS CORAL, *The Times*.

All the . . . skulduggery in the last fifty years has been sponsored by the . . . bookies.

RYAN PRICE, **1974**.

The bookmakers are so intent on murdering the punters that they will in the end liquidate themselves.

HUGH MCILVANNEY.

It seemed like the whole nation had bet on Babur and Goosander for the spring Double. After Babur won, by the day of the National nearly every bookmaker was hedging his money to us.

It was the only time I can remember William Hill coming in to the office on a Saturday. He came up to the Trade Room which I was in charge of and sat down. I said, 'Look Bill, everybody wants to hedge Goosander with us.' He replied: 'When you're laying 6 to 1 a 20 to 1 chance, that's good value. Now's the time to be a bookmaker Sam. Just you get on with it and lay Goosander – don't stop.'

If Goosander had won it would have cost us a couple of million, which was worth a damn sight more than the same sum today. The horse lay about second or third throughout the race, but his face never changed during the commentary. In the end Sundew got up to beat Wyndburgh with Goosander just out of it.

He never turned a hair; just got up and walked out.

SAM BURNS, **1974**.

To beat the bookies you must work at it, then work some more and keep on working. I've been going racing for twenty years and I'm still learning. But the bookies can be beaten.

JULIAN WILSON, *Daily Mirror*, **1974**.

He refuses to accept the assertion that he is a gambler, pointing out that he never plays in casinos, never plays cards and once hired an aeroplane to take him from Manchester to Newmarket on four consecutive days and then never had a bet.

RICHARD BAERLEIN on Alec Bird, **1974**.

The most successful piece of opportunism on the part of Alec Bird definitely came when the photo-finish was first installed in this country. He quickly realized that people were making mistakes about which horse had won in the photo through an optical illusion. In those days almost five minutes elapsed between the time the horses passed the post and the time the photo was developed and the winner announced. This gave plenty of time for backers and bookmakers to do a lot of betting and hedging.

Alec took up a position in line with the winning post and completely ignored the horses. He just looked straight across the course to see which horse's nose passed between the line first. If the one on the far side had won there was no bet, for the public always thought the one on the far side had won. This was an optical illusion.

RICHARD BAERLEIN.

The number one unwritten rule of all bookmakers today is 'Thou shalt not win'. And this is rigidly enforced.

RICHARD BAERLEIN, **1974**.

I must have been in a queue for twenty minutes waiting to say, 'numéro trois gagnant.' Some fools were even saying other numbers. Every ticket had to be punched by the tote clerk. It was past time for the 'off' and I knew that the punching machine automatically stopped when the stalls opened. I'd got half my tickets when it went dead. At the head of a long queue behind me was George Wigg. 'Make sure we never have a Tote monopoly in England,' I said to the then chairman of the Levy Board.

ARTHUR DICKSON WRIGHT, renowned after-dinner speaker, **1974**.

I regard it as criminal the way people pass on so-called tips which, on investigation, have no foundation other than they came from a friend who knows a stable lad, or a postman who lives at Newmarket or a man who gets telephone tips through the post. It is a human weakness to want to confer a favour on another person to inflate our own ego and at the same time give the impression of acting with great generosity.

ROBERT FINDLAY, a Fleet Street sports editor, in *Win at Flat Racing with the Experts*.

Only five per cent of the gate consists of women and, as it is thought somewhat undignified for a lady to be seen betting, they are provided with their own special window.

PETER SMITH on racing in Japan, **1975**.

London was the perfect battleground for me. This was an exhilarating place where you could pit your abilities and your nerve against those of everyone else – because that is what it amounts to, every punter against every other punter – and only the best equipped would survive. I wanted an arena and here was one ready-made for me, with all the elements for testing myself already created and a marvellously varied and fascinating cast of characters.

PHIL BULL, **1975**.

I gave the address at William Hill's memorial service at St Martin-in-the-Fields church in London. An atheist punter giving the tribute to a religious bookmaker – how far can your imagination stretch?

PHIL BULL.

I phoned William Hill one day to complain because I had heard he was closing the account of one of my clients. He asked me to call at his office. I had a great red beard down to my navel and when he saw me I am sure he said to himself: 'I'll soon get rid of this bugger.' The bugger stayed until two in the morning and for the next thirty years I was never very far away.

PHIL BULL.

With betting there is no real article you are selling to a man. What you are selling him is the prospect of profit, or at least the illusion that he may profit. If you raise the tax to the point where you destroy the illusion then you kill his incentive to bet. The Chancellor must be made to realize that betting is a different kind of goose, one that could easily be choked.

PHIL BULL.

Perhaps the most obvious bet was Tanzor to be last. Many good judges made him a certainty and he ran like one, coming out of the stalls like a drugged tortoise and keeping plenty of daylight between the hindquarters of his nearest rivals for the booby prize. Seldom has the form book been so thoroughly vindicated.

HUGH MCILVANNEY on the **1975** Derby.

I wouldn't like to see bookies go, although I think theoretically racing would be better off without them.

JACK MILLAN, **1975**.

To pretend that the bookmakers are not vital to racing is like pretending that the lions are not in Trafalgar Square.

DUKE OF DEVONSHIRE, speaking in the House of Lords.

The British are the most honourable people in the world.

RON POLLARD of Ladbrokes in *Daily Telegraph* magazine.

As every serious punter knows, there is no more chance of the average Tattersalls bookmaker laying a horse to lose £1000 in a bet than there is of him laying a dozen brown eggs.

PETER O'SULLEVAN, *Daily Express*, 1976.

Tatts is a barometer of racing and those who say the only way to do away with doping is to do away with bookmakers are talking complete and utter nonsense.

BRIGADIER HENRY GREEN, head of Jockey Club security, 1977.

The fact that after Tote betting has been available for half a century approximately ninety-five per cent of all betting is at bookmakers' odds must be regarded as conclusive evidence of where the punters' preference lies.

PHIL BULL, the *Guardian*, 1977.

There's no secret about the signs. Anyone could learn them. But a photographic memory is essential in dealing with prices that can change as quick as a flash.

MICKEY STUART, tic-tac, 1977.

Prince Monolulu, bless him, would wave a telegram which had been sent to him, supposedly from a stable at Epsom or some other training centre, giving him last minute information on the yard's runners. The punters would swallow it. The old boy had only sent the telegram to himself.

MICKEY STUART.

The Australian is a punter – there's no doubt about that.

SIR REGINALD ANSETT, Australian industrialist, **1977**.

Fiddling bookies is not crookery, it's making a stand on behalf of the oppressed masses.

A punter quoted by HUGH MCILVANNEY, **1977**.

France has the best racing organization in the world but English racing is knocked down by bookmakers.

MAURICE ZILBER, **1977**.

Years ago, when I used to go dog racing, I had a friend who was supposed to know what was going to win, or rather what the kennel staff imagined was going to win, by the length of lead which was allowed each dog. Dogs on a tight lead were on the job. All I can say is that we followed the system for several weeks and lost a small fortune.

ROBERT MORLEY, **1977**.

A bank doesn't take bets and we don't take cheques.

An anonymous bookmaker quoted by JOHN MCCRIRICK, **1977**.

Tall Mast was the code name allotted to me when I opened my first account with my first bookmaker and that is how I prefer to be known.

ROBERT MORLEY, **1977**.

I remember the late William Hill telling me, as I sat in a Turkish bath in Jermyn Street recording his life story, that in the ten-year period 1945–55 he wrote off £750,000 in bad debts.

RICHARD BAERLEIN, the *Guardian*.

An employee of a course bookmaker was rushed to hospital. Members of his fraternity were quick to visit him carrying small tokens of their respect. The next time they went, there was a large notice over his pillow: 'Not less than £2 taken'.

JOHN TRICKETT, the *Sun*.

A counter clerk at a betting office must be more than a mere disinterested shop assistant. He must be an altar boy in the Church of Gambling. He must know the liturgy. He must respect the rules. He must not laugh because, and Here Endeth the First Lesson, what goes on behind the black glass, is all very, very solemn.

JIM CRACE, *Sunday Telegraph*.

It is hard to be humble when you are as great as I am.

JOHN BANKS, bookmaker, **1978**.

Professionals should not be disheartened when Ladbrokes do not lay them. Instead, they should be perturbed when they do.

JOHN BANKS.

It takes two to make a bet, and the multiples all reserve the right to refuse the whole or part of any commission. I think that morally they should lay the prices they advertise, but there is no legal obligation. If I ask for £2000 these days and get £200 I am thankful even for that.

ALEX BIRD, professional gambler, **1979**.

If ever I discovered that one of my three sons was betting heavily, I would disinherit him.

ALEX BIRD, **1979**.

William Hill was the most wonderful racecourse bookmaker. There'll never be another like him.

GEOFFREY HAMLYN, S.P. returner, **1980**.

Nowadays I'm afraid bookmakers are just glorified accountants.

GEOFFREY HAMLYN.

The modern bookmaker only wants to cater for the small punter who is guaranteed to lose.

RICHARD BAERLEIN, **1980**.

My father taught me that gamblers were much more desirable than sober citizens, for they were always on the brink of winning.

ROBERT MORLEY, *Daily Telegraph*.

Notice that when the boot is on the other foot and it is the punters who are cleaned out, they are not allowed to scream 'fix'.

The reason for this is that, as everyone knows, all bookmakers are born pure and honest, although, as Runyon once said, 'Much as bookmakers are opposed to law-breaking they are not bigoted about it.'

BENNY GREEN, *Daily Mirror*.

Many years ago I was at Leicester when a certain fox hunting peer appeared totally disguised with a beard and other deceptive garb. This did not deceive the bookmaker who had warned him off and the noble lord was ignominiously escorted off the track.

RICHARD BAERLEIN, the *Observer*.

Operation successful but the patient died.

Caption to photograph of Roadway, subject of a major Irish gamble at Cheltenham, being beaten two heads in the County Hurdle, **1983**.

The assumption that the profits of bookmakers ought to be regarded as, in principle, at the disposal of the Levy Board is wholly without justification.

THE ROYAL COMMISSION ON GAMBLING, **1983**.

The implication is that the profits of bookmaking belong in some sense to racing. We do not agree. . . . If the bookmakers prefer to see racing decline and take the consequences that is their business. The same goes for punters. The racing industry is today hopelessly addicted to subsidy. Withdrawal would mean collapse.

ROYAL COMMISSION ON GAMBLING, **1978**.

A fearless gambler is a fool and will always bite the dust. Retain quiet confidence, but beware of certainty.

MICHAEL SIMMONDS, bookmaker, in *Mail on Sunday*.

The privatization of the Tote should rank very high with this Government.

CLEMENT FREUD, **1983**.

I've been chairman of the Tote for nearly seven years. I have not had one letter of complaint that betting has caused a family hardship.

LORD WYATT, *News of the World*, **1984**.

A chap goes there to make a living. You can't tell him when he must bet. There is nothing in the rules covering conduct of bookmakers which require them to open a book at a specific time before a race commences.

REG MCKENNA of the National Association of Bookmakers.

People bet for ego. They bet to boast. They bet so that they can tell somebody they win.

RON POLLARD of Ladbrokes, *Daily Mail*.

I cannot afford to bet.

LORD HOWARD DE WALDEN, **1985**.

The feeling of racing men that their sport is used by bookmakers to make profits is understandable but irrational. There is no more reason for betting on racing than on the level of rainfall (though it is more fun) and the betting business does not in logic owe racing anything.

GEOFFREY WHEATCROFT, **1985**.

When the French take revenge, it ravages the innocent along with the guilty. They do it principally through the murderous inefficiency with which they operate their pari-mutuel system of betting.

HUGH MCILVANNEY, the *Observer*, **1985**.

A friend of mine asked what he would do given the news that

Russia had pushed the button and there were only five minutes before everyone joined the great settler in the sky. Pausing only for a long ruminative pull at a stray whisky glass, the reply came back: 'Tear up my ante-post vouchers for the Classics.'

ALASTAIR DOWN, The *Weekender*, **1985**.

The bookmaker always wins in the end you know. That's why I'm here isn't it?

MARTIN PIPE, trainer and son of a sucessful bookmaker, **1985**.

Never get involved in betting. If you want to live a bit longer, keep off the hard stuff and stick to champagne.

STANLEY WOOTTON'S advice to Richard Baerlein, **1986**.

If you had what I'm owed, you'd be very wealthy.

BARNEY EASTWOOD, Belfast bookmaker, **1986**.

Gamblers are rarely wicked, miserable or aggressive. They have a toleration for others who are not afraid to lose what they have. For them every setback is no more than a stroke of bad luck and every victory a gift from heaven.

FRANÇOISE SAGAN.

Betting is the most moral thing you can do. It is an intellectual pursuit, as good as the *Times* crossword. For millions it is the only uninfluenced democratic decision they take.

LORD WYATT, chairman of the Tote, **1986**.

I know I'm not wrong about a Tote monopoly; it's just too late.

LORD WYATT.

Gambling is against all communist principles.

ALF RUBIN, racing correspondent of the *Morning Star*, **1986**.

It means nothing to me to be the biggest punter in Britain.

TERRY RAMSDEN, owner, **1986**.

No doubt the Jockey Club and Home Office are right that Sunday racing with the betting shops closed would cause some illegal betting. But two questions well worth asking are: 'How much?' and, anyway, 'Who cares?' But let's have no argument, it is worth trying – and as soon as possible, even if a few illegal bookies do make a bob or two. Good luck to them.

LORD OAKSEY, **1987**.

14
Holy Orders

Sunday trading seems such a trivial issue when half our cathedrals are already trading on the Lord's Day.

REV. RICHARD TRUSS, **1985**.

Jesus Christ was not a Conservative. That's a racing certainty.

ERIC HEFFER MP in the House of Commons, **1983**.

Christianity has nothing to do with wild animals. I love dogs, horses and cats but I treat them as such and keep them in their category.

REV. ERIC WHEELER, hunting parson of Steeple Bumpstead, who drove hunt saboteurs out of his temple on Mothering Sunday, **1977**.

The United Council of Churches, in their Report On Gambling, exonerated Terry Wogan completely because they said I tip so many losers, I'm a positive discouragement to people!

TERRY WOGAN, **1977**.

If gambling is within certain limits, a harmless activity, we have no right to condemn it as such.

DR MORTIMER, (Bishop of Exeter) obituary, **1976**.

More people gamble in one way or another than believe in God. The survey 'Gambling in Britain' claims that seventy-six per cent of the public have a flutter while only seventy-four per cent believe in a personal god. Mind you the ones who don't believe in God are taking a bit of a gamble too.

'Sidelines', the *Observer*.

Wanted – Sporting Parson for group of small parishes in Co. Limerick. Stipend not large but rectory with stabling and land available, Box HH 594.

Advertisement, *Horse and Hound*, **1976**.

A Christian is not a killjoy. If he is, he ought to question whether he's a Christian.

DR DONALD COGGAN, Archbishop of Canterbury, **1974**.

I see from the Gloucester and Cheltenham Greyhounds annual report that the Dean and Chapter of Gloucester Cathedral hold almost a quarter of the dog track's shares. Hedging their bets, I suppose.

PATRICK SERGEANT, *Daily Mail*, **1972**.

I don't think that running a betting shop is particularly wicked. I expect I'll be having the occasional bet when I'm at college.

JOHN DEAN, betting shop manager, about to exchange starter's for holy orders, quoted in *The Sporting Life*.

Buying equities to the ecclesiastical mind has all the fascination of gambling without its moral guilt.

HAROLD MACMILLAN, *Financial Times*, **1971**.

Some years ago I had a horse called Ministry so that if the Bishop called when I was out riding, he could truthfully be told: 'The Rectory is out exercising his Ministry.' I now have a new horse to be named. Could your readers make any suggestions along similar lines?

REV. GRAHAM-ORLEBAR, letter to *The Times*.

'Sure, hadn't Saint Patrick backed him?'

Irish punter after Arkle had survived a blunder in his third Gold Cup.

'God put this horse on earth so that we could bet on him,' Andrew Beyer intoned to another writer-gambler one day at Hialeah in Florida. When the horse ran third, the friend muttered that God was, presumably, an each-way punter.

HUGH MCILVANNEY.

> The steed bit his master;
> How came this to pass?
> He heard the good pastor
> Cry, 'All flesh is grass'.

'On a Clergyman's Horse Biting Him', anon.

They're talking a lot of nonsense about the evils of gambling as well. What they ought to be saying is that money is a trust from God, and if a man works hard, keeps his wife and children and contributes to the church, then if he has something over and spends it on the football pools or buys his wife a box of chocolates, there is nothing wrong in that – nothing at all.

LORD RANK, *Evening Post, Hemel Hempstead*, **1969**.

There are of course other forms of assistance, and throughout his ordeal O'Neill, a Catholic, has kept a pretty open line to the top. He explains this with a delightful Irishism. 'I'm not very religious but I'm a great believer in faith.' We were half-way down the fell now, the fields networking away from us across the vale. 'When I was a little better I managed up to here,' he said, before adding with that soft but fearless laugh: 'I thought if I could get this far I couldn't be dying.'

This infectious vitality prompts a final cheeky thought. If there were people like Jonjo about 1987 years ago, is it any wonder where that first Christmas baby was born. Remember, it was in a manger.

BROUGH SCOTT, *Sunday Times*, **1987**.

I have a strong belief in God and I believe that disciplining yourself is a nice way to live. If I miss a day at Mass, I don't worry about it but if I can get there I do.

STEVE CAUTHEN, *Sunday Express*, **1987**.

15
Politicians

Dear Smith,
  I am sure you did your best.
                              Yours,
                              Churchill.

Winston's reply to a letter of apology from Doug Smith for losing a race.

I shall never be a party to such a suggestion [that bookmakers should only be allowed to bet on the racecourse]. Why should I, a staunch upholder of democracy, deprive any man of earning an honest living. I might throw half a million people out of work and I have no intention of doing so.

WINSTON CHURCHILL to Lord Carnarvon.

I do not want to end up my days living on the immoral earnings of a horse.

SIR WINSTON CHURCHILL on why he sold Colonist II.

My mind goes back to the spring of 1949 when Christopher [Soames] persuaded me to buy Colonist. He gave us all great excitement and he was also the forerunner of many successes. I am so grateful to you for the skilful way in which you have trained the horses that I have sent to you from my stud. It does not fall to many people to start a racing career at the age of seventy-five and to reap such pleasure.

WINSTON CHURCHILL letter to Walter Nightingall, on ceasing to be an owner, 1964.

His judgement can be brilliant or berserk; his persistence is endless; his ruthlessness at times too much for others.

WALTER TERRY on Lord Wigg, Chairman of the Racecourse Betting Levy Board, *Daily Mail*, **1967**.

He is incapable of meanness, and he is perhaps the kindest and most compassionate man I have ever known: he'd go on his hands and knees up a mountain to help a pal out of trouble.

IVAN ROWAN on Lord Wigg, *Sunday Telegraph*, **1967**.

He has massive faults. He is impatient; he is intolerant; he is quick tempered; he is merciless to those he regards as incompetent and ineffective if he believes they are taking rewards at the rate appropriate for competence and effectiveness, but he will get up in the middle of the night to bail out the son of some acquaintance charged with a minor offence and spend hours, days and weeks arranging the boy's future and seeking to redeem him from the consequences of some foolish indiscretion.

LORD GOODMAN on Lord Wigg.

Jenkins and Wigg. That's not what I call them. Bonnie and Clyde, that's who they are. These two will kill off racing.

JOHN BANKS, **1968**.

The Chairman of the Levy Board is a man of extreme honour and, like Caesar's wife, is completely impartial.

SIR BRIAN MOUNTAIN on Lord Wigg, the *Observer*, **1969**.

The Jockey Club has told me my job was to raise the levy – that's the plebeian task – for them to reserve the aristocratic job of spending it. My answer was to tell them to go to hell. They wouldn't know what to do with it. They could no more spend it properly than they could raise it, except to build monstrosities I won't mention.

LORD WIGG, **1969**.

The trouble with people who oppose reform in racing is that they are living in an entirely different age. They think that if you haven't got a butler, you don't eat from plates.

LORD WIGG.

I feel like Santa Claus who comes bearing gifts and is hit on the head with a sledge hammer.

LORD WIGG, *Financial Times*, 1972.

Racing once used to be a pleasant escape. Now there is so little friendliness shown towards me and when I finish I want nothing more to do with the sport. Certain people are so damned rude and I don't see why I should go somewhere to mix with them when it is no longer necessary. Emotionally, I just need to get right away.

LORD WIGG, 1972.

It would therefore be a real tragedy if Lord Wigg, who loved racing and betting long before he had any control over them, abides by his declared intention never to visit a British racecourse again. For all I know he may indeed have been roughly treated by certain members of the Jockey Club – but if so he is not alone in that.

JOHN OAKSEY, *Sunday Telegraph*, 1972.

If Randle Feilden and I had been left to ourselves there would have been very few causes of disagreement. But always it seemed he had to go back to an unnamed minority. He was, in fact, a prisoner of the eighteenth century battalions of the Jockey Club answerable to a very small tail on a very big dog.

LORD WIGG, *Evening News*, 1973.

I would wind up the Levy Board. It has served its purpose, but now it is clear that the levy principle cannot be applied on a permanent basis and it most certainly cannot be extended to other sports.

LORD WIGG, 1974.

You learn not that you mustn't get involved in arguments with the government, but that you mustn't get into a flap because the taxi hasn't arrived.

SIR IAN TRETHOWAN, Betting Levy Board chairman, on lessons of a heart attack, **1982**.

You don't bumble up to people like Churchill and Bevan and start passing the time of day as if you knew them intimately.

SIR IAN TRETHOWAN on his early years as a journalist, **1982**.

I hope you never get a Home Secretary who knows anything about racing.

MERLYN REES, former Home Secretary, in **1978**, who was succeeded by racing buff Willie Whitelaw.

I don't know about that. We already have the Toby Belch vote. We must not antagonize the Malvolio vote.

HAROLD MACMILLAN on Rab Butler's proposal to liberalize the betting and gaming laws in the Conservatives' election manifesto of **1959**.

I made the discovery, which came to me late in life, that what was innocent in a Secretary of State was criminal in the First Lord of the Treasury. I do not even know if I ought not to have learned another lesson – that although without guilt or offence I might perpetually run second or third, or even run last, it became a matter of torture to many consciences if I won.

THE FIFTH LORD ROSEBERY.

It is quite true that having sent a horse of mine to run on the Continent, I did so far forget myself as to conform to the customs of the country in which I was staying and allowed him to start for an important prize on the Sabbath day [loud groans from all over the hall].

But, gentlemen, I must add that before I thought about the day on which the race was to be run, I had backed my horse very heavily with the French and I won their money and brought it all back to spend in Scotland.

MR MERRY MP, defending himself against Calvinist criticism, in *Northern Turf History*.

16
Trade

Never bother at all with anyone who isn't interested in racing.

BERT KERR, bloodstock agent, circa **1965**, quoted in *Pacemaker*, **1988**.

I didn't realize I had such a valuable horse until I heard the auctioneer describe him.

ROBERT MORLEY, actor.

As a breed, bloodstock agents are just about one step below child molesters.

ARNOLD KIRKPATRICK, editor *Thoroughbred Record*, **1974**.

I don't know whether I just plain missed his awful legs the first time I looked at him, or something happened between the time I first saw him and when he came into the ring. I apologized, told the boy to take that yearling right out and said, 'Take him home.' Well, the consigner did and named him just that, then put him into training and he won ten races!

GEORGE SWINEBROAD, Keeneland auctioneer, **1974**.

If you are fortunate enough to have some spare cash, go to the sales and wait for the bargains. There will be plenty there – finding them is the difficulty.

MARTIN BURDETT-COUTTS, blooodstock agent, **1974**.

This is one of the quickest dispersal sales on record. This yearling's owner came into racing on Monday evening and he's going out tonight.

JOHN FINNEY, Fasig-Tipton Sales Company's president, after a buyer's cheque bounced, **1974**.

All I know is that I seem to have the gift. I can tell straight away. Anybody who has to keep looking at a horse for a long time to make up their minds is wrong in my book. They'll pull out a horse for me and he'll not be two yards out of his box before I can say, 'We're in business.'

PAT HOGAN, bloodstock agent, **1975**.

School? What was that? I didn't go. At twelve my father took me to the stable of Charlie Rogers. He took a look at me and said, 'Send him up for a couple of weeks.'

PAT HOGAN.

Every other activity at Newmarket was dwarfed by the ridiculous price of 202,000 guineas splashed out by a consortium of owners for a Mill Reef yearling. The sight of two equally stubborn and rich people battling out their eccentricities in public is not one that I find wholly admirable. And as the bidding soared past all sorts of European records the instant reaction tended to be one of sympathy rather than admiration.

JONATHAN POWELL, *The Irish Field,* **1975**.

Conformation, action and temperament. The day you buy is the day you sell. If they are wrong when you buy, those deficiences will still be there when you come to sell them.

DERMOT WELD on buying yearlings, **1975**.

There is only one certainty inherent in a vacation at Saratoga. One needs a vacation when one returns.

ARNOLD KIRKPATRICK, **1977**.

The annual yearling sales, in their own way, are very much a microcosm of the battle of Saratoga 200 years ago. There are the

Gates' and Burgoynes, the victors and the vanquished, both on the track and at the sales. There are the satisfied and dissatisfied, the happy and the disgruntled.

ARNOLD KIRKPATRICK.

The rostrum is a marvellous place to watch from, you know. You see some funny things happen, and, sadly, some rather cynical things as well. But there is no better place to observe human nature.

MICHAEL WATT, chairman of Tattersalls.

New people are students of bloodlines and become astute about them. I tell them to think of the non-tangible commodity - soundness.

ALBERT YANK, bloodstock agent, 1977.

I've bought and sold some terrible bums, but the batting average is good to excellent.

ALBERT YANK.

The night before the Vaguely Noble sale there was a party at the Jockey Club in Newmarket. I didn't have a black tie on and I didn't know a soul. I walked up to a pretty girl with black hair and blue eyes. I said, 'Hello, my name is Yank.' She said, 'I'm Miss Union Jack' and walked away.

ALBERT YANK.

My greatest asset is my eye. I can't hire someone who has my eye for a horse.

ALBERT YANK.

People who can afford a top class horse usually want to run him themselves, not sell him.

ALBERT YANK.

Some people think you're obnoxious if you're a showman, but I have a humour about it. I like to be happy.

ALBERT YANK.

Nothing succeeds like excess.

BILLY MCDONALD, bloodstock agent, quoted by Charles Benson in *Pacemaker*, **1979**.

Call me purveyor of champions to millionaires.

BILLY MCDONALD, **1979**.

He has been engaged seven times and had several near misses, including, most recently, the delightfully named Dallas Sue. Billy has forgotten her surname. Perhaps she needed his.

CHARLES BENSON on Billy McDonald, **1979**.

Not until I branched out on my own as a buyer was I able to prove my point, namely that in horse buying it is one man's judgement which must prevail when the chips are down.

GEORGE BLACKWELL, bloodstock agent, **1980**.

So we eventually saw the horse [Mill House], and all Gollings kept saying was, 'I don't know what you see in him. I think he's a horrible looking brute.'

JACK DOYLE on selling the great steeplechaser Mill House to Bill Gollings, **1982**.

It seems someone has told those guys that bloodstock is the best investment that they can make and so they're falling over each other to spend their money until it's all gone.

BERTRAM LINDER, American breeder, on the booming bloodstock market in **1981**.

Patience is certainly the greatest attribute in buying a horse.

TOTE CHERRY-DOWNES, bloodstock agent, **1982**.

I won't go to Kill because I find the buildings so offensive.

MICHAEL WATT, chairman of Tattersalls, **1984**.

There can be no doubt that Mr Flood bid without the intention of honouring that bid.

MR JUSTICE HURST in finding for Tattersalls on the controversial **1983** yearling sale that was to lead indirectly to the arrest of Lester Piggott.

A Northern Dancer colt went up to $1.3 million before it was pointed out that the animal was a crib-biter. When he went on to make $4 million Cecil turned to Sheikh Mohammed, beside him, and said, 'The man who bought that must be mad,' only for the Sheikh to reply, 'It was me.'

Story told by Henry Cecil during evidence in the High Court, see above.

They're about ten of us doing this for a living, while a whole new crowd came in, have two years at it, lose their brains and disappear.

TIMMY HYDE, breeder, on pin-hooking – the buying of foals to re-sell as yearlings. **1985**.

As far as buying a yearling is concerned, I am quite certain of one thing. As soon as a horse comes out of its box I know whether I am going to like it or not.

LIEUTENANT-COLONEL ROBIN HASTINGS, bloodstock agent, **1986**.

The first thing you look at when judging a yearling is the head and the second thing is whether or not he is well balanced. After that you look for the faults.

LIEUTENANT-COLONEL ROBIN HASTINGS.

It takes a breeder three years to get his horse into the sales ring, but it can take a buyer only thirty seconds to lose concentration and move onto another lot on offer.

JOHN WARREN, bloodstock agent, **1987**.

17

Slaves of the Lamp

Fancy a journalist with racehorses! We shall soon see our 'London Correspondent' with a clean shirt.

Sporting Times, **1879**.

Instead of a month's jail someone should be sentenced to read *The Sporting Life* on non-racing days.

LORD WIGG, *Hansard*, **1959**.

During the past two days I have seen more non-triers at Windsor than I care to remember.

LEN THOMAS, *The Sporting Life*, **1963**.

The larks soaring above their nesting-places on Newmarket Heath this afternoon can be excused for inserting a slight hiccup into their normal exuberant singing-theme when surveying the scene beneath at the second hour after mid-day.

CLIVE GRAHAM on the new starting stalls, **1967**.

> Raymond Glendenning,
> Though not quite sure what was winning,
> Had definitely seen
> That the course was wide and green.

MICHAEL SILLEY in *Yet More Comic and Curious Verse*, on BBC's radio sports commentator of the '50s and '60s.

I did once ask Charles St George how I could become a millionaire and he advised me against trying and said: 'You'd hate it. It's very hard work.' I'm sure he was right. The members' bar is much more convivial than the office.

JEFFREY BERNARD in *The Sport of Kings*.

On these winter afternoons he made his only concession to the existence of commercial television, when he swopped frantically between Sandown on the BBC and Redcar 'on the other side'. He kept a telephone on the floor beside him and dialled constantly, furiously, to lay a pound here, ten shillings there on his 'certainties'. The room was wreathed in smoke; newspapers, carefully annotated, littered the floor; and strict silence was ordained. Never escaping his family's moral tradition, he regarded gambling as a wicked pleasure.

JONATHAN DIMBLEBY on his father Richard as a punter, in *Richard Dimbleby*.

Dear Bastard. You could not tip more rubbish if London Weekend bought you a fork-lift truck.

Letter written to JOHN OAKSEY by a reader of the *Daily Telegraph*.

Top people's tipster Michael Phillips has just returned from a saunter in the Himalayas, or was it a stroll in the Hindu Kush? The prospect of meeting Mandarin on a mountain pass would, I should think, be disturbing enough to send the Abominable Snowman running for cover, particularly if the *Times* man was sporting his tennis shorts.

CHRISTOPHER POOLE.

Thank heaven I'm not a racing tipster. You know how good he is by teatime. City editors get a longer run.

PATRICK SERGEANT, *Daily Mail*.

The danger is that journalists become so involved and so friendly with the trainers, or jockeys, who supply their information that they are loath to report anything distasteful even if it is staring them in the face. They seem to lose their news sense, and for some strange reason, their very standards get mixed up. They forget that in any job their loyalty must be to their employer. It is sad to see the fine writers who really know their subjects and who once were fearless crusaders, now sadly mellow with age so that their outlook is now more that of the Establishment. They can no longer be bothered to unsheath their swords.

TIM FITZGEORGE-PARKER, **1973**.

After Weepers Boy won the Senior Services Gold Cup at York, Peter O'Sullevan wrote, 'I'll go to the workhouse proclaiming that Weeper's Boy's place in the winner's enclosure should have been taken by High Flying, who walked out of the stalls but was flying at the finish,'. . . . Mind you, my fellow wasn't standing still either. I saw him at Newbury a fortnight later and said, 'I read your write-up, Peter. It was fine, but you needn't go to the workhouse, there's an old people's home in Woodstock. I went to see if I could get you in but it was full of your bloody punters!'

SYD MERCER, **1974**.

All men may not be equal on the Turf but Clive Graham came nearer than any man I have known to living his life as though that often contradicted maxim was the truth. Lords or layabouts, bookies or billionaires, tycoons or tic-tac men, stewards or spivs. The status mattered not the least to him. What counted was the man.

JOHN OAKSEY's tribute to Clive Graham, 'The Scout', **1974**.

Ladbrokes sent me a free £5 voucher on the Hunt Cup. I put it on Old Lucky, giving £1 to little Mick, my ward neighbour – it was the name of his small terrier.

We watched on a TV set, close between the beds of two gasping old men, both within half a length of the Holy Ghost. I drew their side-screens and Mick set the TV volume low, so we called Carson home in a bloody whisper!

CLIVE GRAHAM, writing from the London Clinic shortly before his untimely death, **1974**.

There was the time he was leaving the office only to be stopped by the information that he had not done his selections for Folke-stone. 'I picked up the sheet with the runners,' he told me, 'just ticked off one horse in each race and in a couple of minutes was on my way out of the office again.' Two mornings later the *Express* was proudly proclaiming that Clive Graham had gone through the card at Folkestone and, on his return to the office, he found a cheque for £100 awaiting him from Lord Beaverbrook.

TIM FITZGEORGE-PARKER on Clive Graham, **1974**.

Never lacking courage, Clive put his whole career on the line only five years after his entry into racing journalism.

Although always deservedly popular with women, he was essentially a man's man who loved the life of clubs and pubs. At about midnight on the eve of the 1937 Lincoln, long after his big race copy had been filed, he was enjoying a drink with bookmakers Eric Edwards and 'Snouty' Parker when the former stated that he had had a vivid dream of Marmaduke Jinks winning the Lincoln. When Parker commented that he had received some shrewd professional backing for the northern horse, Clive went straight to the telephone and called his editor, the great Arthur Christiansen: 'Throw out the Lincoln lead. Substitute "Marmaduke Jinks will win the Lincoln . . ."'

The sports pages had long since been 'put to bed' but Christiansen, exhibiting his innate flair for the umpteenth time, splashed the racing pages of the late editions with Clive's story. But by the start of racing on a miserable cold wet day the twenty-four-year-old journalist's heart was in his boots. He had committed himself and his paper to a 33 to 1 outsider for the first big handicap on the Carholme.

We can imagine his feelings when Marmaduke Jinks held on by a head to win from Sir Gordon Richards on Laureate II!

TIM FITZGERALD-PARKER on Clive Graham, **1974**.

I have no compunction about spending money, my own or anyone else's. I have very few principles, or at least I try to.

CHARLES BENSON, **1974**.

My father had done so much for me in life and now I found myself telling the bookmakers that when his will came out they'd be squared without trouble. Then the old boy's name appeared in that list that is published in the *Evening Standard*. And opposite his name was the word NIL. It read like a bad football result and it really put the enemy on the warpath.

CHARLES BENSON, **1974**.

I go off the deep end occasionally, but I suspect they think that underneath it all I'm a decent bugger to work for.

OSSIE FLETCHER, editor of *The Sporting Life*, **1975**.

According to his famous son, this unusual father developed an enthusiasm for racing rather abruptly in 1901 at a time when he was given to making evangelical excursions for the purpose of daubing religious messages and exhortations in places where they were likely to be seen by large crowds of people.

On a wall in Doncaster he slapped the question: 'What shall we do to be saved?' Then he found that underneath someone had written: 'Back Doricles for the St Leger.' That joker was presumably the spiritual ancestor of the one on Merseyside who reacted to the Wayside Pulpit's inquiry. 'What would you do if Christ came to Liverpool?' by scrawling, 'Play St John at inside-forward.' Ian St John was a winner for Bill Shankly in his time and Doricles proved no less on Town Moor three-quarters of a century ago. He beat the Derby winner, Volodyovski, after a turbulent race and survived an objection to give a return of 40–1 to his backers, who included a certain travelling salvationist whose search for souls was subsequently less zealous than his pursuit of winners.

HUGH MCILVANNEY on Phil Bull, **1975**.

If you are playing Phil for 50p at snooker you are alright. But when the money goes on it is murder.

RICHARD BAERLEIN on Phil Bull, **1975**.

I'll never lose my love of chess. It is the greatest of games. If I ever went blind, I'd get someone to read to me from all those books on the subject I have studied over the years so that I could re-learn the game. That's how I'd spend my time and, believe me, I'd be quite content.

PHIL BULL, **1975**.

I am personally very excited by every horse race. It is a tremendous spectacle. Each one has something special to it and, as I am naturally thrilled every time, my big problem is to remain coherent and dispassionate, while at the same time conveying my enthusiasm.

PETER O'SULLEVAN, **1975**.

Way back at Withy Grove I remember the chief correspondent was having a terrible run. It was ridiculous the bad luck that hit him. He hadn't had a winner for heaven knows how long and one day the editor sent for him. Everyone knew what it was about.

As soon as the chap got in the office, he took the wind out of the editor's sails by saying: 'Forgive me sir, but do you think that if I knew a good thing on Monday I'd be working for you on a Tuesday?'

TOM E. WEBSTER, **1975**.

My funniest recollection of the Derby, though, was back in 1931. I'd chosen Cameronian and backed my judgement. On Derby Day a salesman brought a new Hoover to demonstrate to my wife. Eileen told him: 'If Cameronian wins I'll have it. If it doesn't you can take it away.'

So there they were sitting by the radio both shouting like mad for Cameronian. The chap wasn't a racing man but I bet he never forgot Cameronian making that sale for him.

TOM E. WEBSTER, **1975**.

I often have people come up to me and ask, 'Why the hell did you tip that thing?', but because I've done my homework I've always got an answer.

JACK MILLAN (Robin Goodfellow of the *Daily Mail*), **1975**.

There's no race I wouldn't nap in.

JACK MILLAN.

If you are a worrier in this game you're dead. I'm just a bundle of fun compared to some people.

JACK MILLAN.

Jack Logan in *The Sporting Life* provokes more thought and high blood pressure than any racing column in the land.

BROUGH SCOTT, *Sunday Times*, **1975**.

A racing correspondent is now a would-be gentleman without a private income.

JEFFREY BERNARD, quoted in the *Guardian*, **1976**.

I've devoted my entire life to painting the thoroughbred racehorse to within a degree of perfection. I don't know why anyone should be able to achieve in two or three years what took me a quarter of a century.

RICHARD STONE REEVES, painter, **1977**.

I write about racing because, unlike football, it has so many colourful characters to offer.

NOEL WINSTANLEY, **1977**.

I have a funny way of looking at things. You would probably call this camera the cheapest I could get. I look on it as the dearest I could afford.

ED BYRNE, racing photographer, **1977**.

His admirers are convinced that had he been at Balaclava he would have kept pace with the charge of the Light Brigade in precise order and described the riders' injuries before they hit the ground.

HUGH MCILVANNEY on Peter O'Sullevan's OBE, **1977**.

I'm probably the only Irishman in history who's never sat astride a horse in his whole life.

TERRY WOGAN, **1977**.

I've even been accused of putting trip wires down, because it was almost miraculous that whenever there was a pile-up I seemed to be there.

GERRY CRANHAM, photographer, **1977**.

Whatever I know now about writing I learnt from the discipline of working for a newspaper.

DICK FRANCIS, **1977**.

One is forced to wonder how much would have been the same if Devon Loch had won; and in honesty I think I owe more to his collapse than I would have to victory.

DICK FRANCIS.

I approach Chapter One each year with a deeper foreboding than I ever felt facing Becher's.

DICK FRANCIS.

Secrecy is essential to British racing, hence the importance of codes for journalists. The last thing they want is for the public to spot them leaving the course after having tipped six losers out of eight, or eight out of eight come to that.

ROBERT MORLEY, **1977**.

Racing over the last twenty years has been uncertain of the fact that it is an entertainment and, like the theatre, it has a duty to entertain the public.

REG GRIFFIN, St Leger Dinner, **1978**.

It is widely believed that there are persons occupied at the BBC with the presentation of sport whose enthusiasm for racing is on a par with that of the Master of the Quorn for hunt saboteurs.

ROGER MORTIMER, *The Racehorse*, **1979**.

He didn't drink me under the table, he drank me under the grandstand.

JEFFREY BERNARD, on trainer Peter Chisman, **1979**.

It's like seeing your horse win the Derby, but carrying the Aga Khan's colours.

QUINTIN GILBEY, on seeing his son, who carried the name of his mother's second husband, play for Eton at Lord's, **1979**.

Legal Paget is there, Legal Joy is there, Dorothy Paget's Legal Joy is there . . . up and over, yes they're all there.

PETER BROWN, amateur commentator, employed by Mrs Mirabel Topham after a copyright dispute with the BBC over the Grand National in 1952, quoted in *Pacemaker*, **1979**.

I have stood in a bar in Lambourn and been offered, in the face of five minutes, a poached salmon, a leg of a horse, a free trip to Chantilly, marriage, a large unsolicited loan, ten tips for a ten-horse race, two second-hand cars, a fight, and the copyright to a dying jockey's life story.

JEFFREY BERNARD, **1979**.

I've got the most beautiful Glendronach whisky. You might call it the Royal enclosure of Teacher's.

PETER SCOTT talking to James Lambie, **1979**.

I don't think I'm ever going to get better, sadly, so I just have to fight against getting worse.

PETER O'SULLEVAN, *Daily Express*.

A good reporter is a godsend to his paper providing he doesn't break too many hearts in the process.

JIM STANFORD of the *Daily Mail*, **1979**.

Parisians are impatient and aggressive. They try and kill you every day in their cars.

DESMOND STONEHAM, French director of the International Racing Bureau, **1979**.

My throat was so dry that I wondered if any sound would come out at all.

PETER O'SULLEVAN on commentating whilst his Be Friendly won the Vernon's Sprint Cup in 1966, in *Pacemaker*, **1979**.

There are so many prima donnas in the game, I think if you tell the truth as you see it you are always going to upset a few people. If you seduced their wives it wouldn't make half so much trouble as if you said something bad about their horses or their riding.

LEN THOMAS, **1980**.

We used to play for the Kildare juniors cricket side, but Paddy [Sleator] got the sack because he would field at mid-off riding a donkey.

ROGER MORTIMER, **1980**.

If I was a newspaper proprietor I would be chary of employing a tipster who didn't back up his opinion in hard cash.

PETER O'SULLEVAN, **1980**.

Christ, I'm going to fall off the f—— roof.

CLIVE GRAHAM's 'sole contribution' to assisting Peter O'Sullevan on commentating the 1950 Grand National, quoted in *Pacemaker*, **1980**.

Racing journalists – and they won't like me for saying so – are the most supine bunch of journalists in the world.

JOHN MCCRIRICK, *Sunday Times*, **1980**.

To begin with I was working down the course and that taught me an awful lot. You see so much that you miss from the stands. Even good racing journalists sometimes say, 'Did you see that one coming home? It was absolutely strangled.' But what they probably missed was that it was being hard ridden four furlongs out and only started to run on inside the last furlong.

MICHAEL SEELY, racing correspondent of *The Times*, **1980**.

The word 'trainer' is also apparently one to be avoided like a dose of equine flu. Widely used descriptions like 'The Wizard of Findon', 'The Master of Seven Barrows', 'The Newmarket Genius' and 'The Sage of Harewood' make members of this sporting profession sound like a cross between professors and prestidigitators.

JOHN KARTER on the descriptive powers of the racing press, **1981**.

In 1972 Raymond Guest's cousin got the BBC to follow L'Escargot, their wonder horse, through his season. It just happened to be the worst he ever had. He failed to win a race!

JOAN MOORE, wife of L'Escargot's trainer, **1981**.

It is doubtful if he could convey the difference between a two-year-old or three-year-old or even a stallion, or indeed visualize two horses fighting out a finish, but when it comes to the flavour of a false start, or jockeys collecting their mounts for a race, he was a master.

OLIVER BECKETT on the painter Degas, **1982**.

The wheels spun round and my smart new car sank slowly into the sand – as Red Rum disappeared in the direction of Anisdale.

JULIAN WILSON on a futile BBC attempt to film the triple Grand National winner on Southport Sands, **1983**.

The recently televised exposure has shown them [the racing fraternity] up in a bad light for which they've only themselves to blame. The TV boys went in as professionals dealing with amateurs, quickly realized that and took advantage of it.

JOE GORMLEY on the Stable Lads Boxing Finals, *The Sporting Life*, **1983**.

The Sporting Life racing newspaper includes a most intriguing personal classified advertisement among requests for stablelads. It offers a booklet giving details of vasectomy operations. Can it be that, with a view to greater efficiency and comfort, there is now a move to geld jockeys?

PETER TORY, *Daily Mirror*, **1983**.

Quite the most nauseous spectacle was the Orson Wellesian figure ensconsed at the front of the Press box, stuffing himself with lobster, swilling vintage champagne and waving condescendingly at the few rainsoaked unfortunates scurrying below whom he chose to believe were his friends.

JOHN MCCRIRICK on fellow journalist Charles Benson, **1984**.

Perhaps the day will come when newspapers will charge the Jockey Club for publishing the race meetings. If newspapers didn't give this information no one would go racing. They wouldn't know what was running.

SIMON 'DODGER' MCCARTNEY on the Ceefax/Oracle fiasco, **1984**. The Jockey Club wanted to charge Ceefax and Oracle a copyright fee for screening race meetings and runners. They stopped showing them.

The French racing press is not as aggressive as it is in England. Everything is questioned in England.

LOUIS ROMANET, **1985**.

There is no reasonable room for doubt that I needed the money more urgently than Sheikh Mohammed.

CHRISTOPHER POOLE on seeing his selection touched off by Oh So Sharp in the 1985 1000 Guineas.

Racing people are a conservative bunch. We are the established paper. It will be *The [Racing] Post* who will need to take our circulation, not the other way round.

GRAHAM TAYLOR, editor of *The Sporting Life*, **1986**.

'That's grand Mr Pitman,' said the security guard. 'But what about your hat?' The beaming commentator obligingly lifted his hat and asked, 'Is there a rabbit or is there a rabbit?' Pitman, for once, had met his match. The guard replied without as much as a smile, 'Jasus Mr Pitman, there isn't even a hair.'

RICHARD PITMAN at Belfast Airport, told by Jonathan Powell in *Pacemaker*, **1986**.

In my lifetime, I have never been less than surprised at the lack of professionalism in the coverage, compared with the depth of detail, imagination and skill you find in writing about other sports, like soccer, golf, cricket or rugger.

CHARLES WILSON, editor of *The Times*, on racing journalism, **1986**.

When the door-bell rang this morning I was sure it was the grim reaper, but luckily it was the milkman.

JEFFREY BERNARD in his 'Low Life' column in *The Spectator*, **1986**.

Give someone half a page on a newspaper and they think they own the works.

JEFFREY BERNARD.

Integrity is all. *Timeform* is sometimes asked by owners to revise its verdict on particular horses, but they get very short shrift. We employ racecourse interpreters. We don't want to hear that a horse won by two lengths. We want to know what it means.

REG GRIFFIN, *Financial Times*.

Bibliography

All the Queen's Horses, Bill Curling (Chatto & Windus)
The Aristocrats, Roy Perrott (Weidenfeld & Nicholson)
Bedside Racing, Willie Carson (J.M. Dent)
Between the Flags: A History of Irish Steeplechasing, S.J. Watson (Figgis, Dublin)
Born Lucky, John Francome (Pelham Books, 1985)
Bred for the Purple, Michael Seth-Smith (Leslie Frewin)
The Captain, Bill Curling (Barrie & Jenkins)
Champion's Story, Jonathan Powell (Victor Gollancz, 1981)
A Classic Connection, Michael Seth-Smith (Secker & Warburg, 1983)
The Epsom Derby, Roger Mortimer (Michael Joseph, 1984)
The Faber Book of Comic Verse (Faber & Faber, 1942)
Far from a Gentleman, John Hislop (Michael Joseph, 1960)
The Fast Set, George Plumptre (Andre Deutsch, 1985)
Five Times Champion, Doug Smith (Pelham Books, 1968)
Flat Race Riding, John Hislop (J.A. Allen 1987)
From Start to Finish, John Hislop (J.A. Allen, 1958)
George Wigg, Lord Wigg (Michael Joseph, 1972)
Golden Miller, Gregory Blaxland (Constable)
Goodwood, David Hunn (Davis-Poynter, 1975)
The Grand National, Clive Graham and Bill Curling (Barrie & Jenkins, 1972)
Great Racing Disasters, John Welcome (Arthur Barker, 1985)
The Guv'nor: A Biography of Noel Murless, Tim Fitzgeorge-Parker (Collins, 1980)
Horseracing – Complete Guide to the Turf (Collins)
Horse Racing in Britain, Barry Campbell (Michael Joseph)
Kings and Queens and Courtiers, Kenneth Rose (Weidenfeld & Nicholson, 1985)

Lester: the Official Biography, Dick Francis (Michael Joseph, 1986)
Lester, Sean Pryor (Sidgwick & Jackson, 1985)
The Life of George V, Kenneth Rose (Weidenfeld & Nicholson, 1983)
Memoirs of Jack Fairfax-Blakeborough (J.A. Allen)
Men and Horses I Have Known, George Lambton (J.A. Allen, 1924)
My Life and Arkle's, Pat Taaffe (Stanley Paul, 19)
No Regrets: Memoirs of the Earl of Carnarvon (Weidenfeld & Nicholson, 1976)
Northern Turf History
One of the Lads, Susan Gallier (Stanley Paul, 1988)
Pretty Polly, Michael Tanner (National Horseracing Museum)
Queen of the Turf: The Dorothy Paget Story, Quintin Gilbey (Arthur Barker, 1973)
Racing Control, Kenneth Stewart (J.A. Allen, 1974)
The Racing Man's Bedside Book (Faber & Faber)
Racing with the Gods, Marcus Marsh (Pelham Books)
Recollections of a Rebel, Boothby (Hamish Hamilton)
Red Robert, Arthur Hearden (Hamish Hamilton)
Red Rum, Ivor Herbert (William Luscombe, 1974)
Richard Dimbleby, Jonathan Dimbleby (Hodder & Stoughton, 1975)
A Rider on the Stand, Jack Leach (Stanley Paul, 1970)
Sods I Have Cut on the Turf, Jack Leach (Gollancz, 1961)
The Spoilsports, Tim Fitzgeorge-Parker
The Sport of Kings, Jeffrey Bernard
Steeplechase Jockeys: The Great Ones, Tim Fitzgeorge-Parker (Pelham Books)
Steeplechasing, John Hislop (J.A. Allen, 1970)
Superior Person, Kenneth Rose (Weidenfeld & Nicholson, 1969)
Timeform's Chasers and Hurdlers 1980/81
To the Point, Woodrow Wyatt (Weidenfeld & Nicholson, 1981)
The Way of a Horse, Marguerite de Beaumont (J.A. Allen, 1953)
The Way the Wind Blows, Lord Home (Collins)
Winter's Tale, Ivor Herbert (Pelham Books)
The Will to Win, Jane McIlvane (J.A. Allen, 1967)
Win at Flat Racing with the Experts, Julian Wilson
The Wit of the Turf, Alistair Urquhart (Leslie Frewin)
The Yellow Earl, Douglas Sutherland (Molendinar Press, 1965)

Index

All horses' names are in italics.